the pain of being human

the pain of being human

by Eugene Kennedy

photographs by Todd Brennan

The Thomas More Press
Chicago, Illinois

Much of the material in *The Pain of Being Human* appeared
in a different form in YOU: The Quest for Spiritual and Emotional Fulfillment, the newsletter written by Eugene Kennedy
and published by the Thomas More Association.

F.S.

CONTENTS

INTRODUCTION

WITH the bitter taste of recent history in his mouth, man has come to associate pain almost exclusively with either sickness or with his own inhumanity. The signature of pain is written large on suffering faces: the shrunken native children whose crusted lids cannot hide eyes that seem a thousand years old; the tragic surprise on the faces of the concentration camp victims in their final experience of deception in the gas chambers; the desperate look of the dying hospital patient searching us for hope we cannot give.

There is, however, another kind of pain in life that has nothing to do with sickness or our sometime savagery. This is the suffering of the healthy person, as undramatic as it is inevitable, as commonplace as it is uncomforted. It is the pain with a thousand private faces, the pain that comes from just being human. No man is innoculated against the ache of his struggle to become himself as a human being and a child of God. Money cannot buy it off, luxuries do not soften it, and no jet plane travels fast or far enough to outdistance it.

Man cannot run away from this pain without running away from himself. He is sometimes ashamed of it but only if he misunderstands it. He can narcotize himself in a hundred ways against it but at the high price of numbing himself to the very deepest meaning of life. Man can only face and deal with it honestly. Indeed, his manner of responding to its challenge becomes the best measure of his maturity.

Healthy men do not experience the struggle to be human as passive martyrs to the nameless fates. In facing the normal pain of life they discover their own inner strength to be free and responsible. A man's best self emerges only when he confronts the truth about his inescapable limitations and longings. This happens when a person senses the ragged boundaries of the human condition as set in space and time. He faces it whenever he wonders, in whatever situation, whether he can make it or not. It is there that he must search for the meaning of faith and hope, the virtues that only come to life when a man is keenly aware of his imperfect and struggling situation. Indeed, it is the quite ordinary effort to believe in oneself and in others that makes men one in the human condition. If shedding each other's blood makes us enemies, sharing each other's tears makes us brothers. Men are linked to one another, like mountain climbers on a steep ascent, in the common struggle to grow and be wise, to learn and to love.

The twinges of life are most keenly experienced in our relationships with each other. We feel them in moments of misunderstanding, in the uneasy times, for example, when a friend demands a loyalty which would make us untrue to ourselves. We feel it when we cannot seem to break through to another and are left alone with some personal grief. Pain is present when we face freedom's choices and we are not at all sure what the right course will be either for ourselves or for others. Pain is there whenever we are challenged really to trust someone else and we are really afraid to do it. This kind of everyday suffering only deepens with the experience which makes us more aware of our dangerous responsibility for our humanity.

Anybody who is really alive recognizes this anguish as the test of our existence. It is compounded of hurt feelings and unfulfilled dreams, of heads dizzied by the pace of our century's change, and hearts scarred by the effort of love.

Fear crackles like fire in every life, fed by the uncertainties that are a constant part of people and events. It is small wonder that men dream universally of desert islands, of quiet and safe places where they might catch their breath for a moment. But there are no such islands, not for any of us. There is only life, unfolding quite mysteriously and with ever-present challenge even in the most commonplace existences.

This is the truth about life which impatient youth, anxious to undo the sins of their fathers, seem sometimes unable to understand. Until they have been stretched a little on the rack of life they will not understand it. Even those most anxious to encourage the visions of the young cannot shield them from the moment in which they will confront their own personal test with real life. It is easy to be brave before this moment comes. But life waits for every person very patiently. Nobody can drop out successfully from the faulted human conditions forever. It is much harder to go on being brave after the first real moment of truth comes into one's life. Part of the pain of life for parents lies in the fact that they cannot protect their children from life, nor suffer it in their place. They can only do their best and set their children free for their own encounter with existence.

What life is really all about flows from the simple experiences of what we are like with those we love. There is no life except in relationship to others, be they spouses, friends, children or pupils. Lovers, who have discovered the only experience that transcends time and space, know a lot about suffering. If they have not tasted the pain of loving, they are not really lovers at all. Even those who love most deeply know the suffering that is sown into all love. There are separations and goodbyes, the tests of growing old and staying in love, the challenges to be faithful and responsible to each other even as life alters them and their circumstances. What nourishes the love of a man and woman long after they have learned each other's faults and failings? What sustains a wife's responsible love for her husband when he is no longer a hero on a white charger in her eyes? What keeps her faithful to him after she knows he will never keep his promises of setting the world on fire, or even getting that long sought promotion? So too, something deeper than romance keeps a man responsible for his wife even after she is no longer young or as beautiful as he once thought. Lovers find faith and hope only when they have faced pain together, the pain that is never completely dulled, the pain that is not an impurity but an essential part of the precious metal of love.

This pain is part of every lover's longing, not diminished but rather heightened by the realization that, in this life, they can never share each other or anything else completely. So lovers rely on each other in a trial of faith and trust that is never over and done with. They understand hope because they constantly make themselves vulnerable through believing in one another. Real lovers never escape the pain of life, but they do conquer the restlessness that betrays the unloving and the unloved. They find peace, and it passes all understanding, because they realize that dying is a necessary condition for real living.

This is the core of the ordinary pain of being human. We learn to yield ourselves up, saying yes to life by saying yes to each other, or we hide from each other and harvest alienation and despair. There is a dying that goes into living with others, a surrender of the self for which there is no substitute. For the Christian this is not just a philosophy of life that says you have to pay for what you get in life. It is instead the very foundation for spiritual fulfillment that flows from our life in Christ. The "spiritual life" is an unfortunately abstract phrase that may suggest that grace touches only some higher and better part of ourselves, or that it is lived only in moments of detachment from the human condition. The life of the spirit is fundamentally lived in our ordinary lives with each other. The pain of life is our share in filling up what is lacking in humanity's participation in the sufferings of Christ. The readiness to die in reaching out in love involves us in the mystery of the Incarnation. This demands a crucifixion, not just a reluctant carrying of our crosses. The pain of being human is not something we are merely called to put up with. Living in the spirit, we are redeemed and redeem each other through an active acceptance of it. This leads to resurrection because it gives us life and makes it possible for us to give life to others.

There is a great deal of talk about the risk involved in loving. This is not, however, a risk that means the outcome will be either painful or pleasurable for us. Suffering is, in fact, guaranteed for anyone who takes on the task of loving. The man who loves will suffer, but he will also find a fullness of life and a personal experience of the Spirit's presence. "What the Spirit brings," St. Paul wrote to the Galatians, "is very different" from the tangled emotions that the self-indulgent inherit. The Spirit brings "love, joy, peace, patience, kindness, goodness, trustfulness, gentleness and self-control." These are, of course, all virtues that describe our relationships with each other, the fruits of committing ourselves to the ordinary struggle to love. Outside of sharing life with each other in the human condition, there is no setting in which these can mean anything.

Man is made strong enough to face hard truths. The hardest is that the healthiest of us come alive only when we are able to understand and affirm that we will always live with pain. Stoicism will never make this truth really bearable. Cynicism will make it completely intolerable. The heart of Christian life is not in rules or rituals, nor in the magic remaking of a difficult world. The Christian, especially, faces the inexorable truth that says that a man finds life only when he is realistic enough to let himself lose it in seeking to love others. Utopia is not the vision that guides him. There is no airy Camelot for the Christian who opens himself to the deepest reality of life's struggle. And he is not a man or much of a Christian unless he understands the pain of being human.

HAPPINESS IS . . .

MEN sometimes make little of the biggest things in life in the hope that their uneasy laughter may hide their deep longing. So happiness has been described as a warm puppy, a dry martini, or the taste of some brand of cigarette. Even these examples point out some of the qualities of happiness: it may arise from quite ordinary experiences and it is very elusive. These things are just clues to man's search for happiness, his alertness to finding it where he can, and his inability to hold onto it for very long. Despite its importance for everybody, we do not have a very good definition of the experience of happiness. We can, however, unless we are completely numb to life, say whether we are happy or not. We also have learned something about the qualities of happiness.

Philosophers and literary men have grappled with the theme of happiness for centuries. Perhaps Goethe, in his version of *Faust*, has told us as much as any of them. In the familiar story, Dr. Faust, abandoning his scholarly but frustrating search for "truth," makes a pact with the devil. If the devil can deliver to him a moment of utter happiness that will cause him to say, "Stay, you are so beautiful," he will deliver his soul to the Prince of Darkness. The devil provides wine, women and song in abundance. These afford pleasure but not happiness to Faust and he is not moved to hold on to these experiences. Finally, as he looks from a hill at the successful outcome of a project to reclaim the land from the sea and as he can hear the joyful sounds of children at play and observe men and women working hard in their homes and shops, Dr. Faust wants to stake a claim on the happy moment and speaks the fateful words. Most of us can identify with some similar experience. We know the yearning to stop time in the instant of happiness even as we know the impossibility of doing so.

Happiness is filled with paradox. To get it, you must forget trying to grab at it directly. Happiness arises as a by-product of our getting absorbed in something worthwhile outside ourselves. It is not necessarily correlated with pleasure. The world is filled with unhappy looking millionaires and restless jet setters. Even the merchants of pleasure seem a glum and lonely lot who are constantly anxious about profit margins and competition. So Hugh Hefner locks himself in his Chicago mansion, a fragile and mechanized pleasure dome that shuts out the real world and seems singularly devoid of joy. And no group seems more joyless than the entrepreneurs of film and stage nudity whose misunderstanding of freedom has enslaved them to a desperate reworking of their compound. Having gone as far as they can, they are more frustrated than happy.

Happiness does not come from a passive kind of peace, the uneasy truces forged with the world through alcohol or drugs. The tragedy-filled world of the flower children has been revealed all too clearly in the last few years. Passivity and withdrawal attract pain and violence rather than peace and contentment. The happy person must be actively engaged with life despite its difficulties; there is no demilitarized zone of disengagement where happiness has no price tag.

Happiness is not self-conscious. It flows from a life of purpose, especially one that is ordered to the service of others. Happiness is bound up with effort and struggle. That is why it shines in the lives of husbands and wives who strive to love each other and their children, even when they have mortgages and other troubles to deal with every day. Happiness does not live independently of sacrifice anymore than real fulfillment of any kind does. Indeed, the Gospel message that the person who is ready to lose his life truly finds it, lies beneath the achievement of any real happiness. The individual who strives to save his life, to lay hold of happiness without letting go of himself, is the one who cannot find it at all.

A further paradox of happiness is that even those who experience it realize that they cannot hold on to it for very long. Life has, as psychologist Abraham Maslow has put it, "peak moments," but these dissolve and a more routine kind of feeling sets in. Happiness cannot be acquired once and for all in this life. The heightened feeling of accomplishment or contentment yields quickly and new tasks and new goals must be undertaken. The person who can acknowledge this is not frustrated, because a deeper wisdom tells him that happiness is not lost forever. Happiness returns as a person recommits himself to life. One of the contemporary enemies of true happiness is the strong emphasis on immediate gratification and the inability of many people to subordinate satisfaction to the sometimes arduous work necessary for its attainment. Instant pleasure is modern man's counterpart of the prodigal son's mess of pottage. For this reason wise men have always spoken of the "pursuit of happiness," rightly emphasizing the purposeful life rather than daydreams of gold at the end of imaginary rainbows.

There are conditions of life that go along with the pursuit of happiness. It is surely the task of every Christian to see that these conditions are available to all men. Happiness is not made for one class, or one skin color. Neither is it something that is reserved for some perfect kind of man who has no flaws in his makeup whatsoever. Persons with great limitations can attain happiness once they have set themselves to overcome them. There are many happy people in wheelchairs who have dealt with the reality of their problems and have overcome them because of their courage and their informed sense of values. So too, man must be adaptable if he is to achieve contentment and productivity. The things that really make an individual happy are quite independent of wealth and circumstance. He can have them available anywhere if he has sensed the real meaning of life. Self-knowledge is, of course, indispensable to this understanding of happiness. The man who knows himself will not set goals that are either beyond or beneath him. He will constantly engage his strength in a realistic approach to life and not demand what he can never achieve nor turn away from what he can really accomplish.

One of the prices of happiness is the fact that it is related to our capacity for deprivation. A person who always has everything he thinks he wants will not be very happy at all. A continued exposure to anything, no matter how good or pleasurable it is, leads to satiety. Hunger, the old saying goes, is the best sauce. And this is true not only of physical things but also of the more profound and spiritual aspects of human experience. Self-denial, a rather unheard of notion even in the Christian world today, is still indispensable to the fulfillment of the person. Even lovers must face separation at times. Constant togetherness can dull the deepest relationship. The joy of being reunited, the wonder of rediscovering each other—these are part of the happiness that is denied to the person who can never deny himself. The latter kind of individual mistakes security and a totally changeless world for the real meaning of happiness. But happiness flourishes on the shifting edge of life where people are ready for growth rather than a static and deceptive security. Happiness abhors a vacuum.

So, too, happiness comes when we are ready to discipline ourselves to give our best effort in life. It flows from concentration and application of one's fullest energies to the challenges that constantly arise before us. Being oneself is a noble ideal but it demands that we make the effort to be our best selves. This is far different from interpreting it as giving some kind of free rein to any and every impulse.

It is hard to beat the Gospels if one is really interested in the achievement of happiness. The Beatitudes are now translated in a manner that catches the Lord's direct address to all those who would follow him. "How happy are the poor in spirit . . . happy the gentle . . . happy those who mourn . . . happy those who hunger and thirst for what is right . . . happy the merciful . . . the pure in heart . . . the peacemakers. . . ." The accumulated wisdom of the ages has not improved on Christ's words. We find happiness when we do not look directly for it but when we give ourselves over to our fellowmen with a willingness to face the pains and problems of life at the same time.

THEY REALLY KNOW
HOW TO HURT A GUY

ONE of the more interesting, if seemingly puzzling, descriptions of human behavior comes under the heading of passive aggression. We are so accustomed to the headlines about direct and violent aggression that we may not recognize, even when it is directed at us, the aggression that doesn't look like aggression at all. Passive aggression describes that psychological mechanism through which we hurt other people by not doing anything at all. This is an indirect but extremely effective form of aggression. It means that by holding back our response (not showing up for a meeting we promised to attend is a good example) we can do more damage than if we tried to express our aggression in a more obvious manner. Everybody finds some of this somewhere along the line in life.

We may even indulge in this kind of behavior ourselves from time to time, pouting or sulking in our tents as a passive response to some fancied or real hurt. It is a form of passive aggression not to talk to somebody else, but we usually know that we mean to be aggressive when we choose this form of relationship. Passive aggression as a psychological phenomenon, however, is not this occasional or deliberate kind of reaction. It is rather a whole pattern of reaction which sprouts from the needs of a certain type of personality and which develops into a style of relating to other people. Passive aggressive personalities are often quite unaware of what they are doing but they do it very well indeed. Like an instinctive athlete who knows all the right moves, the passive aggressive has mastered the moves of subtle aggression. He knows just when to withhold support, just when not to answer a letter or when to drop out so that the maximum effect is achieved. He can look all innocent and say, "I never did anything," but in reality he has done a great deal, letting his own hostility seep out slowly to poison the stream of life all around him.

When we wonder why it is so difficult to get along with another person, the answer sometimes lies in the fact that the other is a passive aggressive personality. These people are extremely difficult to deal with because, although conflict is never on the surface, cooperation is never there either. One of the reasons that it is difficult to help passive aggressive personalities is that the payoff on the unconscious level of their own dynamics is one that they do not easily give up, even when their behavior is pointed out quite directly to them. They can, after all, maintain a rather serene picture of themselves as well-controlled, quite proper and non-violent human beings. They are not, however, peaceful or peace-loving personalities. They are extremely disruptive of the lives of others while they remain remote and inaccessible to healthy styles of relationships. Indeed, the passive aggressive person may be one of the most violent and harmful persons in our whole population, the one who cops out quietly, leaving hurts all around him. In an age of consciousness about direct violence, it may help to recognize this personality type, and to realize the difficulties they cause for genuinely gentle and good people.

IS PRAYER A COP-OUT?

THIS seems like a terrible question, worse even than questioning the importance of motherhood or the American flag. But then even these sacred cows have weathered some harsh seasons recently and have survived. Prayer, however, is always good, or so we imagine. We hesitate to criticize prayer because we see it as the work of the Spirit and believe it to be a grace to find ourselves truly praying at any time. My intention is not to question that very broad category called prayer. Rather, I am wondering only about the sudden and wide-spread resurgence of interest in prayer, houses of prayer, and the experience of shared prayer among priests and members of religious orders. This impulse must be carefully evaluated precisely because it seems to be so unquestionably good. Whatever is truly of the Spirit stands up under close scrutiny; you cannot harm the things of God by inspecting them. The problem is that prayer, along with other forms of piety, is the most socially acceptable shield we have ever known for a retreat from the problems of life.

Our churches, even in that distant time known as the Age of Faith, have always had some people kneeling in them because they were afraid to stand up to what they might find on the outside. Prayer, that heightened relationship of the Christian to God, has more than once appeared in counterfeit form; it has been used by madmen as well as mystics throughout the history of the world. In other words, we may be tempted to return to prayer in our day because, in spite of all our enthusiasm for renewal and for changing the face of the earth, we have found that this world is hard to budge. It is a stark truth that Christian influence is at a minimum in many quarters, even in certain parts of the church itself, and that it is not an easy task to preach the Gospel in the modern world. Prayer looks good when we have played our trumpets but the walls of the world's cities have not crumbled before us.

Longshoreman-philosopher Eric Hoffer put it well: "How easier is self-sacrifice rather than self-realization." It is much more difficult for the Christian to grow into a complete person than it is for him to turn aside and ask God to finish work which seems difficult. There is, of course, no growth in faith at all without the aid of the Spirit. We are, however, just beginning to emerge from an era in which man's lack of confidence in himself severely crippled him—especially in his efforts to become deeply spiritual. Man runs the risk of reverting to a childish kind of prayer when he is frustrated by the severe nature of the challenges of adult living. Prayer by rote, devotions like the good old days, the quiet remove of a chapel visit—these are wonderfully comforting for a person who discovers the difficulties of mature prayer in the face of an unforgiving world.

We need prayer insofar as it defines our lively and true relationship with our creator. God, however, does not disappear if we do not think about him. He will not feel slighted, even if we forget to say certain forms of prayers because we are busy pursuing the works of justice and mercy that he wants done in this world. But aren't these tasks very difficult to accomplish and thus isn't the idea of praying for their fulfillment intrinsically attractive? Isn't that what we are supposed to be doing, praying for all men everywhere? Who can fail to give us high marks in faith if we are saying our prayers regularly? Well, perhaps our new-found interest in prayer demands that we carefully check our own motivation lest this be some kind of cop-out on the Christian works yet to be accomplished in this world.

Real prayer has never been and is not now a cop-out. Real prayer rises out of intense action, like mist from a fast-flowing river. It goes along with and develops out of a vital relationship to a world that is struggling and suffering to make itself whole again. Real prayer never invites us to turn away, not even at a slight angle, from the anguish of the world to which the Gospel is meant to be preached. We are at a new level of maturity in prayer, reaching out together to learn how to pray as adults rather than as those who long for the lost world of our spiritual childhood. The world can be mean, yes, and we have a great distance to go. Along the way, though, we had better be sure that our interest in prayer deepens rather than dilutes our commitment to solving the almost impossible problems of the human family.

HOW DO I KNOW I'M DOING
THE RIGHT THING?

THE hardest questions in life always seem like they should be easy to answer. After all, a man says, they concern the things most important to me and I should be able to respond to them. "What career is right for me?" "Am I really in love?" "What do I really believe in?" When we lay hold of these questions our hands sting at their sharp edges. In the crosscurrents of opinion and confusion, man longs for some degree of certainty. That is why, for the person who cares about life, the overriding question becomes "How do I know I'm doing the right thing?"

This inquiry has been described in many ways over the centuries. For all its mystical overtones, the "discernment of spirits" comes down to the same thing. Every man must struggle to understand whether he is being moved by the Spirit or by some inner whirlwind. It is a continuing challenge to sift the gold of inspiration from the gravel of impulse. It would be nice if a man could do this once and for all in his life. But freedom and choice are a moveable feast, shifting their challenge across the calendar of life from youth to old age. The moment of responsibility for the self repeats itself and the circumstances are always a little different. Man, in other words, must keep on choosing about himself and his life. He does not accomplish this by delaying his decisions, nor by handoff plays that pass the burden to others. Indeed, he is hardly man at all until he confronts his responsibility for his own freedom. That, of course, is what makes it so hard. In the long run each man must answer for himself and accept the consequences. It is so hard that one is not surprised at the resurgent popularity of all the phenomena, from tarot cards to astrology, that supply prepackaged destinies for the human race.

The first thing a man must do, if he is even to phrase the questions properly to himself, is to turn away from the soothsayers and the advice-givers, and to look at himself. This has become an increasingly difficult thing to do. We all develop a picture of ourselves which is resistant to alteration. We think of ourselves in a certain way and we filter our experience, attending to what reinforces our notions and setting aside those things which do not. We like to hold on to the picture we have of ourselves, despite the fact that the evidence of experience may go against it. For example, a man may think of himself as a hard worker. He does not, then, even let himself notice the shortcuts and the longer coffee breaks, the decreased motivation and the skimpier results, which tell him something quite different. The man who sees himself as a responsible husband and father may not let himself notice his own roving eye or his manufactured absences from home.

To face ourselves is to make the real experience of our lives readily available to us. It means that we are sensitive to what is going on inside ourselves. The fundamental source of this information comes from our emotions, the feeling feedback which tells us, better than anything else, what kind of persons we are. When a man asks himself whether he is doing the right thing, he finds the answer by surveying his inner personality. Only if he does this quite simply and honestly can he really deal with his responsibilities.

A person must, in other words, be able to call his reactions by the right names. It is easy to respond to quite adolescent erotic longings and to mistranslate these as a liberation of the self or a new maturity of outlook. To have fancy names for what we do is very handy but it does not alter our basic motivations in the slightest. Indeed, America is full of high-flown rhetoric that justifies voyeurism. It is not surprising that we can fool ourselves about it.

There really is nothing surprising in discovering what our real feelings can be. It is much healthier for a man to recognize his erotic sensitivity and to satisfy it directly than it is for him to call it by some self-congratulating and self-deceiving name and to satisfy it indirectly. He is at least being honest and taking responsibility for what is really motivating him. It is then, as it is with any other personality dynamic, that he can ask whether he is doing the right thing or not. Does choosing this satisfaction fit in with the other parts of my being? Am I really being responsible for my mature growth? Am I satisfying somewhat primitive urges at the price of failing to put myself together as a fully grown man? Does this affect my relationship with my wife and my children?

Am I really being true to my mature possibilities or am I trying to have life all ways at one time?

Here again, a man's feelings, if he has developed a sensitivity to them, will help him with the answer. If his feelings jar against one another, if he cannot really relate all the aspects of his inner self together, then he will hear discordant notes within himself. So too, when a man faces a difficult task, one that frightens him and one that he would like to turn away from, his own emotional response becomes quite informative. I think of a young priest I know who was asked to break the news of a young husband's accidental death to his wife. He was very uncomfortable at the prospect of bringing bad news, of breaking it and having to enter into the sudden grief of the widow. He did not want to do it and he was strongly tempted to find someone else, a relative perhaps, who could take his place. But he took a close look at himself and at the fears that prompted him to turn away from the experience. He inspected, in a few moments, his own reluctance to become involved with pain, and measured it against his obligations as a priest in the particular situation. He chose to go ahead, quite aware now of the sources of his uneasiness in his own fears and quite uncertain that he would carry out his mission well. As he moved forward, putting the feelings of the family before his own, he became aware of a new emotional response which told him he was trying to do the right thing. Afterwards, despite the difficulty of the task and the truth he had to face about himself, he felt integrated. He had experienced a reorganization of himself in response to challenge. He knew now that he had done the right thing because he felt a wholeness in himself, a sureness about his judgment which had helped him to grow in the situation. He was, in a real sense, redeemed through placing his own uncertain and fearful self into a positive response to human need. His feelings now affirmed his move. They also told him that he had been changed through truthfully engaging himself with others.

Every decision is a risky exposure of the self to all the things that can go wrong. The priest might have turned away, or performed his task in a perfunctory and self-defensive manner. Instead, he knew himself well, knew his weakness and his opportunity, and was able to put this real and less than perfect self to the test of life.

This is precisely the developmental sequence for anyone who sincerely measures himself against his challenges. He will be sure he did what was right because he will feel right throughout his being about the outcome. It is interesting to note that this confirming sense of well-being has nothing to do with whether we perform with absolute perfection. It arises because we make our best effort, quite conscious of the difficulties involved and the mistakes we might make, and are ready to accept the consequences.

There is so much of ourselves to take into account in any particular situation that it is clear that no advisor, no matter how shrewd, can really make the decision for us. At this moment of choice, even after all possible information and advice have been gathered, it is up to me. The mature person becomes increasingly sensitive to his own feelings, knowing that, when he is truthful, they will tell him quite accurately whether he has done the right thing or not. This is a world away from impulsivity, the quick giving in to any feelings that happen to come up. These feelings must be tested in relationship to the rest of ourselves and reality around us. Impulsive feelings—to become angry, to cheat, to let other obligations go—must be looked at with care so that their real roots can be discovered. Without a sensitivity to the need for this, the individual experiences no emergent self-control, no integration of himself, no growth and no redemption.

That is why any morality, whether it is called situation ethics or not, is anchored in our own awareness of ourselves in every concrete situation. It is not enough to validate premarital sex or a transient affair by automatically saying that love in the here and now makes it all right. There are more things to be considered when one talks of the presence of all-justifying love. Only the man who is really honest with himself can see if he is using love in a responsible sense or not. He must sense the relationship of this moment's experience to the long-range nature of real love. There are difficult questions connected with this, ones that cannot be put aside, for example, by the fact that the pill will safeguard the consequences of casual lovemaking. The man must ask what this woman means to him, what, in fact, he means to himself and his own possibilities for maturity. Is a passing relationship ever just over and done with? Or does it reflect the kind of man I am, the strength of the commitments I can make, or the direction I give to my life? What does it mean to the other, and what will it mean in the future? How does this affect my responsibility for other relationships in my life? Does being faithful really have value? Or does the immediate gratification that comes here and now eclipse all other considerations? Hard questions, these, and no answers that mean much for the man who cannot listen to his inner self.

The judgment an individual makes about his life has another test. Our decisions can be validated against the experience of the mature Christian community. The so-called laws of morality are really the common perceptions of men and women who try to live life honestly and openly, their common sense of right and wrong. Our actions either fit with the common judgment of good people or they do not. It is easy to fool ourselves here as well, always turning our situation into the notable exception. The experience of the Christian community—not the legalistic or theoretical one —is a consistent background against which to measure our own moral decisions.

SOMETIMES IT'S BETTER TO
LEAVE YOUR MASK ON . . .

. . . EVEN though it is the fashion to take it off at midnight or once Halloween has safely passed. As a matter of fact, one of the most overworked clichés in the age of personalism runs pretty much the same way. People are constantly being accused of wearing masks, of hiding their true selves behind them; the ethos of the age says we are to remove these masks or have them stripped away in the name of more fulfilling relationships. Contemporary salvation comes through self-exposure and there is, of course, something to be said for a right understanding of this. There are times, however, when it is not a bad idea to keep our masks on, times when we should respect others enough to let them keep theirs on too, if they wish.

Although it is good that we have grown to value an honest exchange of feelings, some individuals have made this an intense and humorless personal crusade. They permit no quiver of feeling, no matter how insignificant, to go unexpressed. It is out in the open with everything here and now without delay and without even a bow in the direction of good manners. In the lexicon of the unmaskers, such an attitude is very "real" and very "gutsy." Take off your mask and join the party; let everybody know what you really feel about them and everything else. This usually consists in telling others how you dislike yourself and/or them. It means playing it as it lays in this age of personalistic confrontation.

Any real sensitivity to human relationships, however, dictates that there are times when we should keep masks and our feelings firmly in place. The very fact that we experience and recognize certain feelings does not mean that we must express them. Our emotions are not churning around just waiting to be siphoned out publicly in a raw and unprocessed state. That, however, is what some people want when they drop their masks and urge you to do the same. Life is all feeling, without a forgiving smile for one's foibles. Few understand that feeling, important as it is, is only a part of human life.

There are many occasions when we must keep our feelings under control for our own sake as well as for the sake of those around us. We don't have to play life with a poker face to recognize the wisdom of moderating our emotional responses. If we just let go with some primal burst every time we are frustrated, crossed by another, or hurt by something in life, we will soon self-destruct. If we want a response to our feelings now and cannot tolerate any delay, we will go through life like babies who respond only to their impulses. Sometimes it is hard work to keep ourselves together, difficult indeed to maintain the mask of control when we want to rip it and scale it away from us.

So, maintaining ourselves is important for our own stability and growth; it is also important for others. We cannot let our feelings fly when there are those around us who either cannot handle such onslaughts very well or who would be deeply offended by our determined honesty. We must, in other words, keep a mask on our feelings whenever we would otherwise make ourselves a burden to others. And that covers a wide variety of situations, from remaining calm in the face of disaster to keeping our courage up so that others won't lose theirs.

The masks we preserve in these situations are not phony cover-ups for our real selves; sometimes they are the better side of ourselves, the side that is only revealed when the pressure is on and the stakes are high. It is clear, however, that the person who lets himself go emotionally is living in response only to his own feelings and that he is incapable of taking the feelings of others into account. Despite the claims of the passionate unmaskers, revealing all your feelings all the time is not adult but childish. And besides, some of us look better with masks on anyway.

THE WORST THING ABOUT PAIN . . .

. . . IS that it doesn't kill us; we never die of pain, although we sometimes wish that we could, if only to put an end to it. And the worst pains are those which seem to have no remedies, the ones that tear the edges of our spirit because they come when we are healthy rather than when we are sick. We may try to tranquilize these pains away, but eventually the ache returns. They even go on vacation with us, waiting for an idle moment or a familiar song to use as an entrance into our hearts. What is this pain that will not kill us, this ache that has learned how to follow us so closely through life? It is the pain of being alive, the pain of always having to face a new challenge, the pain of wanting love (and the pain of finding it), the ache of starting again when we don't feel like it, the tension of coming to terms with a life that keeps shifting under our feet.

There are a lot of simple old cures for this kind of suffering, some of which we have forgotten in the midst of our new-found friendship with tranquilizers and sleeping pills, and in our ability to purchase a kind of friendship in psychotherapy. The oldest antidote is to shake ourselves loose from our passivity, to face down the inclination we have to play Camille in order to get a little sympathy from ourselves if not from the crowd around us. Like the old country doctor's remedies, compounded from a wisdom that still endures, the old-fashioned idea of pulling ourselves together is not really half bad. Perhaps we have grown enamored, in late twentieth century America, of brooding over the stresses of our lives, of counting liabilities more than blessings, of waiting for love rather than loving. In fact, that last stance may well be the key to a much better handling of the pain that hurts but does not kill. Giving, despite the hoarfrost on the cliché, still beats getting; it's about as therapeutic as anything we know. And if we are persistent, this course of treatment not only makes us feel better, it leads us to real loves as well.

Lent has an old tradition of self-inflicted pain in behalf of the expansion of the spirit; we used to almost enjoy forty days of purple and penance. That's all gone now; the spirit of Lent is doing something positive these days, and that, of course, is all to the good. But instead of trying to dull it, suppress it, or just avoid it, perhaps we could take on the source of our worst human ache this year. We might let ourselves feel it, and then organize ourselves so that this suffering no longer holds a secret kind of domination over our days. Some things, the poet tells us, are too deep for tears; but a real effort to do something positive for Lent might focus our attention on getting ourselves together enough to grow stronger in the face of the pain that is too cruel to kill us. And there are all kinds of things to do that will help to bring us out of ourselves and into a fuller life. This is not an invitation to stoic striving as much as a call to bolder Christian living. We can do more with our pain than suffer it, and the world needs lovers more than martyrs. The point is, of course, that the pain really *won't* kill us and that we should not let it keep us from reaching out to others just because that is the way we got hurt in the first place. This Lent let's have another go at it; our pain will grow less as our hearts grow larger. We conquer the slow death of pain by a full try at life.

A LOSS OF FAITH

"FAITH," a reflective priest friend once said, "is what you run out of in life." He put into words a feeling that all men know well, even if they cannot describe it for themselves. There are times when things pile up and one's spirits sag, dark hours when a man wonders if his strength has not been mined out at last. He has been running the race, he would like to finish the course, but can he possibly keep the faith?

Faith under stress does not immediately refer to a man's willingness to accept some particular formulation of dogmatic teaching. It means something more fundamental, something deep in his being, his very capacity for any kind of belief at all. This is in the core of personality, the ground of his relationship to God and man. It can seem suddenly eroded and uncertain, a terrain illumined by lightning flashes of weariness or disappointment which make it seem too terrible to travel any further. That is when man feels overwhelmed, struck numb by doubts about his own or God's power to help. It is a desperate feeling and a man experiences great loneliness in the face of it. Life looms up as a weighty challenge, neither asking nor granting ground, pressing its demands when one feels least capable of meeting them.

There are many faces to this assault on faith. A husband and wife wonder at times whether they have the energy to keep on believing in one another, whether they can continue to respond to one another for better or for worse. They need faith in each other and in God precisely at moments when they seem to have the least amount of it left. There is something absolute in the act of trust they make at times like these; absolute because all other emotions seemed drained away; absolute because if they cannot count on each other they can count on nothing at all. Their sighs tell us how much they feel the burden of each other. The honeymoon is long past and nothing is certain about the future. Strength seems to come only from moment to moment and understanding is hard to generate. But somehow, it is in facing this experience together that they communicate what they could never say in words to one another. They have shared a desperate moment as deeply as they have shared more happy times. The important thing is that they really shared something, even when there seemed precious little left to share.

I have seen many priests and religious in great pain about their future. Perhaps some of their closest friends have gone and with them the warmth and memories of less clouded times. The Church seems a world filled with warnings. The prospects of renewal they were counting on appear deferred to an unborn generation. They have faith in God but they have little faith left in the bureaucratic aspects of Church organization. They examine the fiber of their faith and they are not sure that it is strong enough to hold together much longer. Can they really believe enough to trust the Spirit? Or should they seize what is left of life and try to salvage something of comfort for themselves? These are dark and difficult questions and they are not put to flight by the reassurances of a retreat master. For some these are questions they never thought they would hear themselves asking. It is a sore and aching time for them, especially when they want to do the right thing, when they want to serve and not just save themselves.

This anguish is not different from that of parents who know they must believe in their children if they are to help them to grow, but who find the steady investment of their care and attention increasingly difficult to make. What world have they made for their children, and how can they blend trust and concern in such a way that the child is neither abandoned nor overprotected? The Church itself seems unsteady, in conflict rather than peace, a source of concern as much as a source of support. They cannot help wondering about the sacrifices they made for the faith with such confidence at an earlier time.

All these situations are painful because nobody speaks any magical or soothing words. There is just life to be faced and borne with whatever reserves one has left. The experience is so common in our day that we might weep for recognizing each other in it. At these bleak far ends of life we find and can redeem each other. It is not a question of one or the other of us having all the answers to clear away the doubts. It is not that some charismatic figure will provide a previously untried spiritual nostrum that will invigorate us. The truth is, as it is for husband and wife, that in opening ourselves even a little bit to each other, we get the strength that comes from sharing something very real about life. We are truly in touch with each other and that is an increasingly rare experience in the great, slick pop culture that tends to make us competitors rather than friends. Our culture specializes in surfaces, whether these are television screens, high fashion, or the smoothly styled shells of automobiles. It markets allegiances, whether to baseball teams or brand names, but it does not provide much in the way of sustaining faith. This only comes from experiences in depth, and these are found in our relationships with each other.

Sustaining faith is what we human beings can give to each other. If we do not share enough of life at the times when we feel sure of ourselves, we can find something real to share at those moments when our faith is weak, even if it is only our own emptiness. We are ourselves with less than the usual pretense when our confidence is shaken. We are more open to each other and also to the Spirit. Maybe it works because we are so genuine, so appealingly human, so much in need of each other at these times.

For many people, this is one of those times. They need the rebirth of faith that comes from the response of other humans. "How can I believe"—the old question is as fresh as ever—"unless some *man* shows me?" The renewal of ourselves, the restoration of our trust, is mediated by our relationship with others. Faith doesn't fall from the skies; it comes to life in our human experience. It is in sharing with others that we sense the meaning of the Church as a people, the supporting community of those strengthened by the Spirit.

When faith is under strain it is not revived by a new pronouncement by some official nor by resolutions passed by some organization. Its renewal depends on how willing we are to be a sharing and trusting community, a body of believers ready to believe in each other. The depth of the faith of the people of God is clearly related to how much they actually are a people together, persons on the same pilgrimage in whose caravans there is room for all.

It is interesting to note that when St. Paul wanted to strengthen the faith of his fledgling communities, he reminded them of their obligations to help each other in a very personal way. They had heard the Good News, he says over and over again, and now they must share life together. "You should carry each other's troubles," he writes to the Galatians, "and fulfill the law of Christ." And to the Ephesians, just as clearly, "Be friends with one another, and kind, forgiving each other as readily as God forgave you in Christ." The measure of our faith, and the sign of our participation in the mystery of the Redemption, is our willingness to reach out to one another, even at the price of letting our own weakness be revealed in the process. It is the fundamental trust involved in this self-revelation which builds our own and our neighbor's strength.

The times when faith is on trial offer Christians the opportunity to be the Church by being a People together. God does choose the weak things of the world because that is the way that most of us are; we can glory in that weakness because it makes room for the action of the Spirit. Pride, an unfashionable but very real entity, shuts the Spirit out because it shuts us off from relying on each other. The present tensions only become unbearable when we sentence each other to suffer alone.

LISTENING TO ONESELF

IF man wishes to communicate effectively, he must learn how to listen. This insight is nowhere more apt than in a man's effort to communicate with himself. Self-knowledge, that precious metal of spiritual and personal growth, is not mined easily. In fact, people sometimes dig for it in the wrong places, with the wrong tools.

Twentieth, going on twenty-first, century men find it hard to listen to themselves. They are literally under siege from the artillery of communications, from the big guns of the mass media, the pop guns of gossip-communists, and the sharpshooters of cocktail parties. In the midst of all the noise, men find it increasingly difficult to hear what is going on inside themselves. It is small wonder that they accept willingly the made-to-order opinions about what they should be like, whether these come from the *Playboy* advisor or their local preacher.

If a man wants to understand himself, he must take the soundings of his own depths. He does this, not by asking what he thinks nor even what he believes, but by asking what he feels. A man's emotional life is not some independent sub-system that operates according to random rules. His emotions tell him, as nothing else does, the kind of person he is. His feelings are an integral part of himself. They provide an accurate indication of his reactions and his values in the face of the experience of life. Beneath his feelings, the feedback mechanism of his personality, lies the real man or woman. The person who listens to his feelings is really listening to himself with all the facades and pretense stripped away.

The person who can begin to hear what his feelings are telling him gets at the roots of his being. "What are the things that get me mad?" "What are the things I am touchy about?" "When is it that I am so shy?" "What are the things I would make sacrifices for?" "What are the things that embarrass me?" "What are the things I feel sure about?" The answers to these kinds of questions yield a profile of ourselves that is truthful even if it is sometimes difficult to look at. Indeed, it is so painful for some people to face and to take responsibility for their real selves that they prefer to leave their destiny to the astrologers and other currently fashionable soothsayers. The truth may be hard but it is more reliable than the zodiac as a basis of life for truly human beings. The truth alone frees us to be ourselves. We are very uncomfortable in life until we are ourselves.

When a man begins to hear what his feelings are telling him, he begins to understand himself. He can, with a little reflection, and sometimes with a little help from another person, get to the bottom of his feelings, and thus to the bottom of himself. Unless a man identifies his emotions correctly, he has neither self-knowledge nor self-control. He is instead, whether he knows it or not, controlled by his emotions. Although he may hide this from himself by denying or disguising his feelings, he does not thereby alter their influence on him. Sooner or later, in direct or indirect fashion, what is really going on inside himself will break through. Suppression of our inner dynamism never really works with great effectiveness. The man who denies his anger and frustration at work will manifest it at home. The individual who does not deal openly with his sexual feelings will symbolize them in subtle ways in other behavior.

In short, the whole complex of man's feelings is never successfully drowned out by the surface noise of life. They remain present and affect his behavior whether he wants to acknowledge it or not. The person trapped by his emotions is the one who has not learned to face them squarely. Control is exercised only by those who can hear what their emotions are telling them and who are ready to enter into them both to understand and control them.

The first step toward maturity depends on our readiness to find the quiet place in life where we can genuinely listen to the fascinating messages about our identity which our feelings constantly whisper to us. It may only be a first step, but no other step to fullness of spiritual or personal growth can be taken until this one is made.

GETTING SOME OF OUR PRACTICE
INTO THEORY

THAT, according to a priest-missioner friend of mine, is what life is all about these days, and there is a lot in what he says. Not only is this a stimulating reversal of an old phrase, it is what we do most of the time in life anyway. Anything that is worthwhile comes about in this manner, because what is ultimately durable has deep roots in everyday experience. Theories come along to explain the facts of life; they do not invent them or determine them beforehand. The great legal geniuses of history have not imposed regulations on human beings out of the blue. They have taken a long look at man and the way he does things and they have written laws by distilling the best of living experiences.

In a way, getting our practice into theory is what the renewal of the Catholic church is all about. The greatest suffering in the religious sphere of life has always arisen, like a science-fiction creature out of his movie tomb, from trying to make people live and believe according to what comes out of the head of a pastoral theorizer who is removed from the human condition. Men may make an effort to force themselves into somebody else's formula for living but sooner or later it breaks down. Most rootless theory works the same way—as anybody who has ever tried to assemble Christmas toys can tell you. The man who wrote the instructions has clearly never had to assemble the toy. And so it is with all those men (and the world has seen too many of them) who want to tell you how to live.

But what really works in life, even in the most intimate and sacred aspects of our actions with each other, comes from experience. The very word "moral" comes from the Latin word *mores* which means customs—the standards of behavior that have developed in the lives of good people. In the long run, experience speaks to experience, and man finds the moral way when he discovers the way that matches rather than contradicts his own nature. The rules of good morals, then, take their shape and force from the fact that they represent the wisdom that men have achieved in trying to do their best in relationship with one another. The theologian, traditionally the last one to hear what is going on in life, puts into words the common judgments of men who try to live by the Spirit. But he does not invent virtue; he learns to describe it so that we can better understand it ourselves. The best measure of our own behavior is not to compare it with some theoretical paragraph in a textbook. We should test what we do against the behavior of good people who are not trying to fool themselves about their lives or their obligations to each other.

All the authoritative books that have ever been written on this subject come down to this idea of getting our practice into theory, of seeing that the fundamental Christian experience has its basis in what we do in relationship to each other rather than in some prepackaged system of morality. The latter phenomenon is the kind of thing you find in environments, be they churches or countries, where the people who are in charge have a need to control the behavior of others according to their own whims. But that is not Christianity, and it never has been. For the Christian is called to be free and honest in living his life and facing challenges, to do his best by himself and by his neighbor. He knows that the Spirit is found not in the clouds but in our commitment to the experience of everyday life with each other. And the man who understands that really doesn't need much theory anyway.

THE MANY FACES OF LONELINESS

MEN are made brothers in many ways; some by blood, but more still by sharing the same human experience. When we laugh or are afraid together we form bonds that help us recognize each other as members of the same family. It is hard to look on another man as a stranger once he has revealed his humanity to us. Strangely enough, one of the experiences that draws men together in understanding is the loneliness they feel when they are separated from one another. And separation is a strand woven into all human experience from love to death. No man escapes it, no man can solve the problem by himself, and no man who has ever been lonely can fail to be touched by loneliness in another.

This is not just the loneliness of alienation, although this experience is common enough in our day. Even in the Church, people on both sides of the generation gap know the pain of suddenly feeling like strangers in a land no longer to their liking. The different generations talk separate languages and look for different sources of religious comfort or strength, but they know the same pain of feeling caught somewhere between the older order and the new.

Nor is the loneliness only the deep and brooding withdrawal of the mentally ill whose own darkened and fearful worlds open painfully if at all to the approach of friends. This may be the starkest loneliness because it is so hard to touch even with the warmth and compassion of true friendship. The mentally ill can seem so locked away at times, longing for human companionship but unable to open themselves to it. This can generate a special loneliness in the family, friends, and even the healers of the mentally ill. They feel outside the other, limited by the illness from giving themselves in friendship even when this is what they wish most to do.

Loneliness is not just the aching void that comes into a family when one of the members dies, although the depth of this feeling is unmatched by many other of life's experiences. This is loneliness indeed for the widow or the widower, a loss that faith alone can overcome through the sudden vista of years where one who had walked so closely with another must now walk alone.

Loneliness is all of these things and it is more besides. There is a loneliness for the healthy person that arises in far less dramatic situations, loneliness that man cannot wish away or neutralize with distractions. It comes and goes and, could we sense it in each other, we would be closer and more tender to each other.

There is, for example, the loneliness that a man experiences when he knows more than his comrades. The prophet is not only without honor in his own country, he may also be without friends. If a man sees clearly the reality of some issue before his companions can, he will pay a human price for his insight. He will have to live alone with his understanding and with the strange isolation that such knowledge brings.

There is also the loneliness of the person who is misunderstood and who cannot seem to communicate his real feelings to another. This man wants just to share something that is bothering him with another human being. But, strangely at times, there does not seem to be anybody else around who is really ready to listen. Everybody is too busy or too preoccupied with his own problems. Or perhaps the other person misunderstands, as is so often the case even with those with whom we are closest, and the result is a numb sense of being left alone when we really want to be with somebody else.

There is the loneliness that creative people must find and face if they are to share their vision of the world with other men. They must, it would seem, draw apart from life for a while if they are to get life into their work. But this experience is painful, and well nigh incommunicable. Without this pain of being alone in the discipline of his art, the writer or painter cannot really be anything but a copier of other men's works.

There is the loneliness that goes with waiting, and life seems to be filled with waiting for so many people. It is the daily round for the housewife, waiting for the children, waiting for her husband, waiting in doctors' offices, outside schools, and beside railroad stations. It is a loneliness of expectation and a loneliness of drudgery and it is as common as the rain.

There is even a special loneliness for lovers, for those who know most intimately the joys of sharing their life and struggles together. This comes at the many times when they must be apart, or in the moments when they realize how much they want to share and how limited they are in ever sharing completely the best of things in the human condition. Real lovers are not lonely because they are unloved; they know the unique mystery of separation that is heightened precisely because they are loved deeply.

"Loneliness," Thomas Wolfe once wrote, "far from being a rare and curious phenomenon, peculiar to myself and to a few other solitary men, is the central and inevitable fact of human existence." This is the loneliness that draws us together in the human family.

Loneliness reveals a good deal of our true selves that lies hidden within the more crowded house of life. Our strengths and weaknesses, our values and our ability to take charge of our own lives—these show through when we are, for whatever reasons, alone for a while.

Some of the mystery in the separation of those who love each other echoes through the Gospels. Christ separates himself from his family, he draws apart from his friends, he allows himself to feel deep loneliness in the Garden of Olives, and he baffles his apostles when he reveals that the necessity of his leaving them is intimately bound up with his redemptive mission. Christ's departure from his closest friends is necessary if the Spirit is to come to them. "You are sad at heart because I have told you this. Still, I must tell you the truth: it is for your own good that I am going because unless I go, the Advocate will not come to you; but if I do go, I will send him to you."

The climax of Christ's life, in his crucifixion and death, is a shattering moment of separation as he leaves his loved ones humanly desolated. It is this moment of separation, when Christ allowed himself to feel so alone and uncomforted by the Father, when his mother and friends were left to know the depths of loneliness, this moment of the separation of Christ's Body and Blood that is remembered in the Eucharist. Each experience of personal aloneness or separation from those he loves reflects the Christian's participation in the ongoing redemption of the world.

We have not been left orphans and the Spirit does come to us when we can see our multiplied loneliness as a reminder of the Christian vocation and as an occasion for the coming of the Spirit.

In the loneliness we must all face we can sense our need for each other. We live in Christ and are made one by the Spirit when we recognize loneliness as something more than a random evil. It is rather the opportunity for us to face its challenge and to reach out with love and understanding to each other. We can find each other in loneliness and do something about it through the power of the Spirit.

It is not, of course, easy to face and deal with the many faces of loneliness either in ourselves or in others. It is much easier to pass each other by, or go about our business, and to leave the loneliness of mankind unredeemed. It is, however, also our great chance to bring the Gospel to life. This demands a willingness to look into each other's lives, not curiously but compassionately, not to meddle but to share ourselves in the many moments when this is the only gift we have to offer each other. The fact that we have tasted loneliness and understand its relationship to the Christian life gives us the human base to be a source of salvation to each other. In the loneliness we all know, we become our brothers' keepers.

THE MAN WHO PLAYED PEOPLE
AGAINST EACH OTHER

HE seems like a nice guy; they all do. He is very earnest, apparently intelligent, and seemingly quite a gentleman. He has the social skills and the sophisticated smoothness that come from squeezing his way through tight places. He does rather well on his own strange path through life until people begin to compare notes about him. This is the man who gets ahead by playing people off against one another, the master of the game that the late psychiatrist Eric Berne described as "Let's you and him fight."

There have been other cultural descriptions of this slippery person but, whether he is making the snowballs for other people to throw or suggesting softly the words for other people to speak out loud, they all get at the same truth. Down deep in his heart he is the classic double agent whose only loyalty is to himself, the man who makes his way at the expense of other people, the non-hero who always shows up in the eye of the hurricane, dry and warm while the storm rages around him. Part troublemaker and part self-aggrandizer, this character is so skillful at playing people against each other that he is frequently the last person suspected of being at the bottom of a certain problem. He can look quite innocent and so disinterested but, if you look closely, there is blood on his hands that he can never wash away.

Why does he act this way? Somehow or other he has learned he can get ahead this way, he has found that it can be rewarding, and so he makes it a kind of career. Playing both ends against the middle becomes a style of life that he masters, and it seems to pay off. He learns, as John Heywood wrote, "to hold with the hare and run with the hound" and this technique works at least for a time. But as Lincoln said about not being able to fool everybody all the time, this person trips himself up with his own fancy footwork. His success in playing people off against each other is based on their fundamental goodness; his downfall comes from their ultimate common sense.

Sooner or later people begin to question the man who seems to be on so many sides of a question, and so much at the bottom of intrigue and dissension. The divisive crack in human relationships, when we trace it back, always leads to his door. His very cleverness in dealing with people makes him a success and a failure at the same time—a success in that he may get the big promotion and all the money, a failure in that he isolates himself from the rest of men in the process. The tragedy is that although it may take a long time to suspect what he is truly like, the day of reckoning finally does dawn. And it finds him an empty and confused person, looking for self-justification or trying his old tricks only to learn that people neither believe not trust him anymore. Playing people off against each other is like discovering fool's gold—a cruel and finally self-defeating illusion. So pity the poor man who makes his way through life in this fashion, but don't let him fool you while you're feeling sorry for him.

LOVE'S MOMENT REMEMBERED

LOVE lasts, St. Paul and our own experience tell us, but we have never taken this truth as seriously as we should. Love endures, carries on its effects in us, and continues to be powerful well beyond the moment or the relationship in which it is experienced. Love is not like food that provides temporary nourishment but does not permanently stay the rhythm of hunger. Love gives us strength that remains with us because it adds something to us that does not ebb away of itself. It changes us because it makes us grow and there is no going back on growth that has been achieved. Love that we have really known from another lives on in us even when the other has left us through death or separation. It is like a fire in us that burns brightly to light our way and warm us for the days when we are alone or under stress. It kindles our own motivation and our own power to love; we can keep giving love away without losing any of it.

We think about love in very limited ways and we are too intimidated by the songs and stories that speak only of the desperate fear of losing love. We even limit the possibilities of experiencing it when we are so dominated by the fear of its slipping out of our grasp. That is not the way of real love, which is made of far more durable material. It is, however, the way of the many inadequate and substitute notions of love that plague us. That is the love we try to demand of another as an account payable, or the wish of love that is merely a passing attraction or the echo of our own need.

There is a great mystery about real love that has never been captured by poets, artists, or sentimental preachers. It is solid and deep, a miracle far more common than visions, or wonders, a wonder in itself that cannot be bartered or put safely away, like gold, in some cool private vault of our personality. Love does not seek a hiding place; it demands expression and it craves sharing with others. Genuine love is active, its dynamism undiminished by the passing of years or the shifting of circumstances. It is, of its essence, creative and so it gives and sustains life. It wants to be out in the open where it can grow and spread to others.

Christians, least of all, can view love as a perishable commodity, or as something that must be locked away from life itself. And the most unacceptable notion of all, if we take the Gospels seriously, is that love is dangerous. It is powerful, yes, but it is not dangerous. It flourishes in those who can face the problems of loving and the hurts that life can inflict. The real danger exists for those who never want to face these things and who never experience any real love at all. It is a strange thing that so many Christians are shy about loving and so unwilling to open themselves to it, or to let others open themselves to it. They choose rather to build walls and fences against the supposed dangers of love, and so they do not know the moment of love nor its continuing power. They are the lonely ones who will not let themselves understand that real love casts out the haunting danger to all life, fear.

There is a mystery in love because it breaks down walls and topples over fences. It does not confine itself to one relationship or one style of relationship. Love is found in many places and we would not be afraid of it if we really believed in the Gospels. This is true because any love that is selfless is the work of the Spirit, the action of God in our lives, the evidence we can know that supports our faith and our hope. Because it is the sign of God touching our lives, it is powerful and creative. As Father Robert Johann has written, those who have loved have been given "a glimpse of the world beyond care."

The most distinguishing mark of lasting and creative love is found in the sense of responsibility that goes with it. This is far different from the hit-and-run tactics of those who use other people for a while and then put them aside. It is a world away from those who play at loving others with glowing phrases and a mastery of the manipulative arts. It is meant to last and so it imposes a telling discipline of its own, a discipline that flows from a sense of being responsible for the other in season and out. This means that a real lover is committed to the good of the other and not just to the satisfaction of his own need. It suggests that a genuine lover wants the beloved to grow; only the counterfeit lover wants to control the other in all the aspects of life.

The lessons of loving are not mastered all at once. Sometimes it takes a lifetime of learning and perhaps we must settle for the human condition of getting better at it as the years go by. This too is one of the effects of real love because it matches the way men are and helps them to continue the process of growing out of themselves. That is why love lasts and enables us to learn to share it even with our enemies. The Gospels tell us all of this, just as they tell us that it is never too late to respond to the Spirit of love that can so transform our lives.

It is often the remembered moments of love that keep us going beyond the imagined limits of our own strength. When love is real it is powerful in the mark it makes on us. It enlarges us and moves us always forward. Love's inherent strength makes it more powerful than death or any of the hazards of life itself. Love is what Christians should be good at so that the whole world can be strengthened to put away its fears.

Men have always wanted to leave something lasting behind themselves. Only the mighty or the highly gifted have the chance to do this through history or the arts. Everyone, however, leaves something that outlasts the greatest fame or accomplishment when he reaches out, even for a few moments, in loving another. He touches the ways of all men and their destiny when he can love one man with deep responsibility. He becomes an instrument of life, ever-increasing life, when he truly loves. His name may be forgotten but the presence of the Spirit survives in the love he leaves behind.

ON LEAVING PEOPLE ALONE

THE catalogue of misfortunes inflicted by humans on each other in the name of love is large indeed. Throughout the course of history people have done the most astounding things to each other, always with the energetic reassurance that the sole motive for the action was love. This begins early with large spoonfuls of bitter medicine held firmly in reportedly loving parental hands; doctors and dentists lulling us into an innocent vulnerability with promises that "This won't hurt a bit"; the father of the family administering some heavy-handed discipline to a soft-bottomed child with the unlikely protest that "This hurts me more than you."

It is a part of wisdom to understand that people who love each other often must allow each other to suffer at times. Life must be faced and the pain is made tolerable only because someone else does love us and supports us through it, even when he or she cannot prevent it. This understanding is found between husbands and wives, and between them and their children; friends know this experience as well. It is not easy to let someone you love suffer a crisis of growth, an illness, or a trying experience at school or at work. But lovers face these things all the time and redeem each other through entering into them together.

Far different from this, and distinctly nonredemptive, are the people who move into the lives of others with plans for remodeling them. Like amateurs who try to remodel anything, they are confused about their purpose, their motivation, and their skills. They frequently end up causing a good deal of damage. This is exactly the case with the meddler who flies the banner of love as he charges into the inner precincts of another person's personality. He calls his destructive foray by the name of love, and he manifests his misunderstanding of love in a wide variety of situations. You see it in the busybody who has plans for your perfection and is always willing to share them with you. There is the person who has long range plans for your life and attempts to force them on you. Boldly assertive are the individuals who want you to respond emotionally to them and who manipulate you, even to the quoting of scripture, to get you where they want you. Familiar too are the enthusiasts for some particular form of prayer or supposedly spiritual experience who absolutely insist that you join them. Worst of all, I suppose, is the individual who inserts himself into the relationship of two other people with the supreme self-confidence that his loving intervention will help the others to be better in some way or other.

There is no denying the usefulness of friends who are truly interested in us and who do love us enough to confront us with either our shortcomings or our unfulfilled possibilities. That, however, is not the kind of friend I am describing here. The meddler can be easily recognized for several reasons. First of all, he is basically insensitive to himself and to other people. He has a short supply of insight to match his ardor for interfering with others. Most prominent in his make-up, although perhaps unsuspected by him, is the role his own needs play in his relationships with others. He is not seeking the good of the other nearly as much as the satisfaction of some drive or need of his own. He will not admit this, of course, and to cover it he invokes the notion of love. This is why he is so harmful to others; he gives love a bad name because of his superficial understanding of it.

The core difference between the meddler and the lover lies in the selfishness of the former and the selflessness of the latter. A real lover puts himself and his own needs to death for your sake; a real meddler closes in. The lover, even when he is leaving you to your own pain, prizes you; the meddler, even as he may be causing you pain, is first in his own affections.

Real love, as St. Paul wrote to the Corinthians, is really very understanding. It does not seek itself. Perhaps he could just as well have written that real love knows when to leave other people alone.

THE PSYCHOSOMATIC SIGNS OF HEALTH

AMERICANS are forever taking their own temperature, checking their blood pressure, and keeping a wary eye out for the signs of illness. It is not an uncommon experience for a person to read about a vivid account of the symptoms of some disease and then to find himself experiencing these very things himself. The imagination plays a large role in the self-inflicted terrors of these phantom pains and aches. In fact, Americans have become somewhat sophisticated in understanding the meaning of psychosomatic illness. They realize that the uneasy stomach and the blinding headache may have their roots in unsettled emotions rather than in some fault in their physique.

All these developments make us very conscious of the signs of distress and strain in our physical makeup. It helps create the market for home remedies and endless self-medication. Perhaps it would be good to focus once in a while on the signs of good overall adjustment, the symptoms of psychosomatic health.

The biggest sign of the healthy person is a lack of self-consciousness about himself. He is absorbed in living and is not carried away by concern for his well-being in any neurotic way. Indeed, good adjustment is not self-preoccupied. In the healthy individual the physical and emotional aspects of man's unity as a person are integrated. The healthy person fits together well and a general feeling of well-being is the result.

A further symptom of health is that the individual is productive. He reveals a certain zest for living; there is a spontaneity about him in his work and his relationship with others that is not a forced gaiety but the realization of his real creative possibilities. When well adjusted, he meets his life and work with a healthy enthusiasm and anticipation that provide him with the energy to carry on.

A healthy person is creative in many ways, even if these are in situations and efforts that are not related to the arts. There is an element of creativity in the healthy housewife, the busy priest, the interesting teacher, or the good neighbor. Creativity is not always dramatic, and it is an unproven notion that it only arises out of some kind of mental illness. A fresh approach, an ability to see things and people in a new light, a task done with pride—all these are signs of creativity in more customary settings.

Close and affectionate relationships with other people are possible to the healthy person. Once again, this need not have excessively dramatic overtones. Reliable friendships, the ability to trust, the willingness to share oneself with others are commodities that come in different sizes, but their source is in good adjustment. The reason for this is that the well-adjusted person is able to love himself properly and so can bring his true self into relationships with others. One of the sure signs of this is his ability to receive love and trust as well as bestow them. Only the unhealthy person, the one who lacks self-esteem, cannot offer his true self to others, cannot afford to receive their affection in return.

Adequate self-knowledge enables the healthy person to accept himself the way he is. This means that he is aware of his feelings and the reasons for his actions and does not distort them out of some neurotic need. The healthy person can assess his strengths and his weaknesses, knows what he can do and what he cannot do; he therefore sets realistic goals for himself. He neither overestimates nor underestimates himself in the face of life's tasks. That is precisely why he is productive.

Perhaps, in a world full of bad news, it might be a good thing to pay attention once in a while to the soundings within us which affirm our strength in the human condition. None of these characteristics is possessed in absolutely perfect form by any of us. They are, however, the kinds of experiences of the self that well-adjusted persons possess in greater or lesser degree. Loving ourselves properly includes a willingness to accept the good things about ourselves without making a big deal out of it. That is the best sign of all of our good health.

BUT I DON'T FEEL LIKE IT . . .

WELL, most of us do not feel like doing many of the things which life flings in our paths during the course of a day. And it is not just old-fashioned wrong-headedness or an unredeemed Puritan ethic that motivates us to do things in spite of the way we feel. Oddly enough, however, as the great pendulum swings back from the over-rationalized emphasis of a previous era, Americans are redis-covering their feelings—and they are responding to the messages they are receiving with varying degrees of maturity. Right now the measure of decision, commitment, being faithful, doing one's job, and half a dozen other things has come to be whether and how intensely a person feels about it.

Our feelings, of course, are good guides to action but only when we are willing and able to go beneath their surface to trace down and sort out the tangled roots of our various impulses. Emotions are not very dependable guides in the lives of persons who are un-prepared or incapable of this kind of self-examination. Neverthe-less, many people readily accept the first signals of their emotions; they make no effort to understand why the feeling is there in the first place. This response, impulsive and undifferentiated, is all they need to set their course for the day or the week. In a way, this attitude is not very different from the response of the child who, when he is urged to do something, "doesn't feel like it"; a long process of learning about himself must intervene before he con-sciously alters that answer. When an adult responds in this way, it suggests that he has not passed beyond the child's level of self-comprehension and that his absorption with his own small world of feelings keeps him an exile from mature relationships with the larger world around him.

Allowing vague and ill-defined feelings to rule us is a far cry from the grown-up individual's unself-conscious capacity to re-view his own emotions as he makes one decision or another. But self-examination is a difficult task, one that requires searching honesty and self-discipline as well as the ability to balance one's own inclinations against the rights and needs of other persons. Duty is not a dirty word for such a man; it is not neurotic to tackle distasteful chores. The adult is no stranger to his own faint-heartedness in times of challenge or his own queasiness at the prospect of fulfilling a difficult obligation, but he does not cop out when he heads into the contrary winds of his own emotions. The mature person is not afraid to integrate clashing feelings and to let his own desires take second place in the order of action. The mature man, perhaps a dozen or more times a day, does things that in some way or other he does not feel like doing. That is to say, he is grown-up rather than hung-up on making the universe spin around his own personality.

Christ himself was not surprised to discover and deal with reluctant feelings at various occasions described in the Gospels. You can sense his drawing himself together in the face of obstacles, not in some super-human manner, with the unflinching plastic control that some evangelists attribute to him, but with the realization of crosscurrents within himself. He had to deal with many feelings— from sadness at the death of Lazarus to desolation in the Garden of Olives. Christ was obviously aware of the many levels of his human emotions, but he had a sense of their interrelationship and of the hierarchy of values that guided him. A little death goes into every reordering of our own feelings at those times when, if it were left totally up to us, we might say the hell with it. But those kinds of deaths of self give life to the full-bodied maturity of the man who is not afraid of facing a life filled with things he does not feel like doing.

TEMPTATION

IF ever a notion has become old-fashioned, it is that of temptation. It still hangs, like a darkening daguerreotype, in the Christian gallery, but it seems more the evidence of a historically
interesting process than the representation of anything real.
Modern, free-flowing moral forms, in which self-discipline seems
an enemy, catch all the attention these days. The current cultural
code not only allows but commands a response to any and every
impulse. The notions of delay of gratification or the control of
one's inner stirrings are judged to be puritanical residue at best.

This supposedly free and easy approach to drawing water from
all of life's wells may, as many observers contend, be a kind of
overreaction in the present to the overcontrol of the past. There is
a lot of talk about how a man must do everything and taste every
possible experience, if he is really to be alive. Indeed, as a concept,
temptation is associated more with the perils of affluence than the
building of character. It is invoked in the presence of the rich
foods and the richer dessert carts that threaten the contemporary
slim look; it is manipulated skillfully so that men end up buying
what they cannot afford in order to give the impression that they
can afford it. There are many reassuring slogans about living a
little, spoiling oneself justifiably, and about how long we will be
dead that help make it easy for us to deal with temptation, according to the formula of Oscar Wilde, by yielding to it.

Temptation is not dead, however, even though the word may
not be used much any more. Temptation is a real experience, no
matter what name we choose to give it, and it still gives rise to
tension, restlessness, and conflict. It is by no means limited to the
area of sexuality, although it is real enough there. The struggles
of temptation are also felt by men who crave, among other things,
power, money and influence. Our old picture of temptation posed
man, full of yearning, before some forbidden fruit. He either gave
in or backed off; he conquered or was conquered. Although this
is still accurate enough as far as it goes, it leaves out a great deal

that is important for a new look at an old problem.

Temptation, in a sense, is not all bad. It should be viewed as part of man's struggle for growth, an aspect of life experience that is essential for his full development. Every man must test his own identity against reality itself. An individual does not grow merely by thinking about it, or wishing for it; somewhere along the line he must measure his self-understanding and his strengths in the contest of life. None of the vital steps to maturity, such as the acquisition of impulse control, can be taken unless a man subjects himself to the tension of making a choice, which is the most important sign of a free man.

To eliminate temptation is to close off one of the avenues that lead men to fullness of personal development. The worst result of those modern-day thinkers who would have man do whatever he feels like whenever he feels like it is that this robs man of choice. It despoils him of what is most human about him, his freedom to choose for himself the values by which he will live. And every man born to be responsibly free will have many temptations, even when he doesn't want them and even prays to be delivered from them. The tautness that a man feels inside himself at the high tide of temptation arises because the real issue is always the nature of the choice that he makes. In fact, temptation does not always run at flood tide through our lives. However, a steady flow of choices, some big and many small, are presented to us every day. It is not just in the heightened moments of temptation but in all these decisions that man can choose himself. He can choose something that will add to his growth, or he can choose something else that may detract from or delay his growth. A man does not choose himself once and for all; it is an act he must repeat every day in many different circumstances and the temptation to choose something less than his full self is always present.

Perhaps that is the underlying meaning of every temptation no matter what the specific setting. We can choose what makes us bigger or what makes us somewhat less, whether it is a question of failing to tell the truth, or of cheating at our job, or even cheating on our spouse. The primary temptation asks us whether we love ourselves enough to do right by ourselves, whether we will tap our full potential or sell ourselves short, whether we will possess ourselves fully or let ourselves go. The way we respond to ourselves in the moments that test our strength tells us, better than anything else, whether we have any sense of responsibility to others. We end up either giving them more of ourselves, and this means growth, or of giving them less of ourselves, and this comes close to the real meaning of sin.

The temptations of Christ are illustrative. In essence, they were invitations to put aside his vocation, to relinquish his sense of mission and all its possibilities, and to settle for power rather than service. Man is always fundamentally tempted to give up what he can really be, to withhold himself from life and thus to deny himself and others the effects of his full self-affirmation. We can hold back in subtle ways, in friendship for example, or in love, where the demands of faithfulness are put into sharp focus by temptation. The temptation is always for a short-term gain and the forsaking of a longer-range commitment, for something of the instant that imperils something more lasting. Moments of temptation ask us whether we are ready to grasp and deal with the deeper values connected with the self and the meaning of life. These are never easy moments and we can deftly defend ourselves against facing the truth about the many issues involved. We can, in other words, live at the surface of life, never getting into or sharing our true selves with anyone. That is the destructive core of temptation, the slow shrivelling of the self that has never entered into life at all.

Wholeness comes to a man not just from resisting temptation, although this has traditionally made him feel good. An individual grows when he faces the full dimensions of temptation and chooses the course that demands more of himself. That is what helps him to sound his own true depths and to release his true creative powers. We are fulfilled not, as some contemporaries suggest, by giving in to temptation in the name of fuller human experience; nor are we fulfilled, as some ancient spiritual writers seemed to suggest, by backing away from life and its dangers, frozen in some pious attitude of resistance; we are fulfilled as we find ourselves through making positive choices that demand more of ourselves. Temptation is an opportunity to make a commitment to one's better self, to one's possibilities for the fullness of life that is promised to all Christians.

Our reaction to any temptation offers a moment when something essential about the Christian dynamic of life is represented.

We die to something in view of a richer and fuller life that follows from self-affirmation. These are redemptive moments that recapitulate the whole of Christian life, and ask us to choose it even though it causes suffering, because resurrection inevitably follows. The Christian is a free man and each temptation gives him the chance to proclaim this truth over again.

TWO THINGS YOU CAN'T DO WITHOUT

THERE are two qualities or conditions (call them whatever you want) that are essential for the most important things in life. Oddly enough, however, they are also the two factors which some people count as enemies and spend their lives maneuvering to overcome. A man does not need wealth, comfort, or even good dreams to get him through life; he has even less need for fame or good looks. What he cannot do without, however, in his most vital experiences as a person, are freedom and time. Nothing that is humanly worthwhile can be accomplished outside the demands that these qualities impose on all of us; and yet they are also the realities that frustrate man the most. There are those who would limit a man's freedom; sometimes he even does it himself. And there are many who are unfriendly to time, uneasy and never at peace with the clocks that measure our days.

You cannot achieve anything of value unless you invest it with freedom and allow it the kind of time it needs fully to develop. All the things that season a man's character—love and trust, friendship and faithfulness—must come freely through the medium of time or they do not come at all. All life moves toward freedom, toward a healthy and responsible independence that is achieved only by those who commit themselves to a participation in the sacred mystery of time. Nothing that is ultimately good comes in chains or outside of time.

Even lovers whose hearts beat to a timeless pulse and who long for unity must finally work out their relationship in freedom and patience. In patience, we are told in the scriptures, we shall possess ourselves. So it is for lovers who, anxious to lose themselves in each other, come up against the reality that they can never completely do this, and that the miracle of love exists only for people who recognize and respect their own separateness. Kahil Gibran tells us that true lovers learn that there must be spaces in their togetherness. Lovers come close to breaking the barriers of time but time reasserts itself and has its way with them.

They cannot conquer or tame its effects with makeup, or fool themselves into thinking they have escaped at jet speed. A life worth living is one worth growing old in; lovers learn that doing this together gives full growth to their love.

It is surprising that we rebel against those forces which are always with us, forces that are essential for a fully human life. People, however, want to control their lives and program their futures at the high price of eliminating all surprise. Worse than this, some people want to control the behavior of others; this is the great temptation which comes, I suppose, to every man who has ever loved anybody. He would like the beloved, in some wild and impossible dream, to remain unchanged, to stay forever youthful or forever innocent. Parents can wish this for their children, teachers for their pupils, and sometimes even lovers for each other. This hint of the desire to prolong youth goes against the whole thrust of the human condition; it is a vain and betraying wish in the lives of those who try, in one way or another, to carry it out. A person may wish the one he loves not to change so that he himself will not be hurt by the changes that will inevitably come if he truly allows his beloved to be free and subject to the measure of time.

A double vulnerability is involved in letting people be free and allowing them to have their own lives in their own time. They may disappoint us or cause us pain because they use their freedom poorly or because they grow old when we wish they would not. We are, then, prompted to over-protect our children or isolate our loved ones from any opportunity to taste life itself. But controlling the lives of others or attempting to eliminate the necessary conditions of life are strategies that almost always diminish rather than enlarge the possibilities of the other. What individuals need most are the kind of freedom in which we stand by them and the kind of time which we are willing to enter into at their side, so that they can find and live by the truth of their own personalities. Freedom and time can seem like masters to us if we are afraid of them; they are on the side of those who have truly learned to love.

That is the problem with people who have no patience with the good things that insistently demand an investment of time. They want things immediately and the delay of gratification seems sinful to them. What is it, after all, that you can have right away in this world of wonders? A radio station that, thanks to the miracle of transistors, comes immediately to life to tell you the news that you have already heard two or three times before? A television set, bursting into color at the touch of a dial, to show you a rerun of a game show? Man's marvels of communication only make life more painful, seeding him with a greater yearning rather than satisfying him. The things we can have instantly are often shallow and insubstantial, commodities that cannot last and that quickly dissolve the very quality of time they have tried to overcome.

What is timeless and lasting is a life to which we give ourselves freely in the knowledge that we will have to learn to deal with time if we are going to live as God's children. There are a thousand deaths involved in tackling life on its own terms, yet this is the way to go deeper into life and to discover there the richness and the values of loving and believing that outlast all the clocks of the universe. The Christian commits himself to the human condition, acknowledging his mortality, and exposing himself to the hazards of real living that are understood by those who are afraid of freedom and time. Gospel values are eternal but they are rooted in a feeling for freedom and time. The Gospels are full of the talk of waiting—waiting for the seasons, and waiting for the harvest—rather than hurrying things beyond the tempo of their inner promise. Coming alive is not accomplished in an instant; grabbing at it only betrays those who, despite their bright banners and balloons, have never learned to wait. As the Christian enters life he accepts the responsibility of freedom and the penalty of time. Eternity offers the realization of the other side of freedom and time, that is, life to the full sealed forever against the vulnerabilities of our human passage toward it.

PROPHETS ARE WITHOUT HONOR . . .

. . . THEY say, at least in their own country. But why is that, I wonder? Why, especially in an age so fascinated with the future, should people turn their prophets out to pasture and send their seers into exile? Wise men nod and tell you that it has always been this way and that there is no known cure for this malaise which has been fatal for so many who attempt to tell us what is to come. The cure is elusive because mankind has a habit of wanting to believe only good news about the future even though many relish scandals and bad news in the present. Men have been killing the messengers of bad tidings for a long time now and prophets, because they bring bad news as well as good, are not much fun to have around.

The prophet is guilty of talking about things as they are, of describing reality as the collage of good and bad that it necessarily is; that is why he is unfavored by the people who do not want to see the world as it actually is. Prophets are not magicians, readers of tea leaves, or searchers of the stars. They are the persons whose fundamental good sense and vision allow them to see deeply into people and events; they can imagine well what people will do in the future because they understand them in the present. A prophet knows what will happen because he understands the probabilities of human reactions. Human understanding, as any beleaguered government planner can tell you, is a far better guide for the future than growth curves and economic "game plans."

Well, that all sounds relatively harmless; no need to get upset over a man with human insight. Therein, however, lies the rub, and also maybe the best way to tell a false prophet from a true one. The false prophet does not have the integrity of the real prophet; he puts on a good show but he is fundamentally self-serving. The authentic prophet has too much integrity for that, so he just says what he senses to be the truth because he feels an overriding commitment to his own clear view of things. And this is exactly what gets him into trouble wherever he may be found, whether in the church, business, or public affairs. The prophet who knows what he is talking about deals in truth, not fads. He dares to put into words what most people, deep down inside themselves, are afraid to acknowledge as true. They do not want to face the truth because it is too threatening to them; it means they will have to change and they are not ready for that at all. So it is easier to turn things outside of oneself, to project one's anger about an unfolding truth on the person who is brave enough to speak it for the first time. The prophet is not honored precisely because his vision of the way things are is too frightening, too demanding.

This is what Jesus did in his preaching and why he was such a threat to the stultified religious establishment of his day; we are threatened by anybody who summons up the implications of our hardened hearts and human ways. They make us uneasy, not because they tell us about some science-fiction possibilities (the kind of acceptable and distant truth we swallow enthusiastically) but because they tell us what is really occuring in our own lives and our own times. Such men are dangerous because they take away our illusions and fragment our pretensions; they simply don't let us get away with anything. Men can forgive other men for many things but no one ever seems to forgive another for being right when he himself was wrong. Hence the difficult state of the prophet in his own country arises when he overturns cherished defenses simply by knowing what he is talking about.

You can find real prophets in any walk of life: in businesses that would rather fail than accept the truth about the future; in armies and navies that want myth more than reality (remember Billy Mitchell?); and in churches that preach harsh sermons but dread hard truths. Maybe we should try to make life easier on the prophet wherever we meet him. Of course, listening to a prophet would mean that we would have to be ready to change ourselves, ready to recast old beliefs and to integrate new aspects of reality into our world view. Adapting might be quite hard on us at the start but it could be very beneficial in the long run. And prophets, when we have the courage to listen to them without keeping up our guard, really know something about the long run. The prophets who are very self-conscious about their predictions are very anxious to control our lives. They confuse rather than enlighten us, but the world listens to and regards them because they generally tell people what they want to hear. There is something of the "yes man" and the snake oil salesman in the false prophet. But in the true prophet, in the man rooted so deeply in the truth that he knows the direction in which it is taking us all, there is something of the wonder of what man can be.

FAITHFULNESS

THE present climate of our country offers little encouragement for the faithful person. Indeed, the man who tries to keep his commitments as best he can must get discouraged at times when he sees infidelity, in so many forms, rewarded. The non-hero, the adulterer, the deserter; we have found reason to praise them all of late. The real question must be: why are men faithful in a culture that fails to reward it?

It is not easy to remain faithful to one's wife, one's responsibilities, or one's convictions, when the world makes it easy for us to put them aside. There are many signs of this, for example, in connection with marriage. Recently, in books and articles, we have seen an increasing emphasis on the positive aspects of infidelity. An affair outside marriage, some people say, is good for the marriage, or at least good for you, and not necessarily harmful to the marriage, especially if the other partner does not know about it. So too, moralists are becoming more tolerant of infidelity and are saying so publicly, even as they note the danger of generalizing about such matters. Lawyers have come to the concept of the "no-fault" divorce so that adultery is fast disappearing even as a legal entity. Add to this the reported change in the attitude of women about these concepts and one can understand the pressure the person who struggles to be faithful must feel.

Much of the glorification of extra-marital adventures comes from clever but superficial minds. Publicists and philosophers of the "good life" do not have to pay the price for the kind of behavior which they encourage in others. Neither do other social observers or moralists who, on frequently shaky kinds of data, find good things in unfaithfulness. They are removed from the anguish of everyday life, and they seem at times quite insensitive to the widespread signs of man's longing for some affirmation of faithfulness. This comes across, among other places, in the women's magazines where hardly an issue appears that does not contain one or more articles that express a woman's uneasiness about the faithfulness of spouses in marriage. It comes across in the cries of youth who are searching, as much as for anything else, for some adults in whom they can truly believe. They protest an elder generation's infidelity to itself and its commitments. That is why the key word in their slogan about those over thirty is "trust." It is hard for them to trust people whose behavior seems to them to be marked by too many sellouts to forms of infidelity.

It is striking that the world has so little to say that is positive about the concept of faithfulness. Perhaps it has lost hope because it has known so much in the way of disappointment. It is surely here that Christians have something to say and something to show to the world. If, as psychiatrist Leon Salzman has noted in his extensive research on infidelity, there is always some failure of commitment, some lack of real love involved, it is clearly a Christian obligation to offer a better understanding of these things to mankind. Underneath all the glorification and pseudo-sophistication, infidelity flourishes where people have forgotten how to love each other, and have given up the sometimes difficult work of staying in love with one another.

The Christian who tries to live by the Gospels offers the world some insight into what is demanded of those who would spend a lifetime together. Love, when it is understood as a process of growth that includes joys and pains, is a distinct challenge to the concepts of instant gratification and "Let's not make any claims on each other" that are currently fashionable. The most revolutionary thing a Christian could stand for is not a bloody uprising against the establishment, but a real belief in the meaning of love. That is not easy, because it demands that people continue their search of themselves and of each other, that they continue to listen and to grow in relationship with each other, even as age and circumstances work great changes in them. It is getting easier all the time to give up when a relationship finds itself in difficulty. People who buy this philosophy gradually find that there is no center of gravity in their lives, that their identity is a smear, and that their restlessness is not quieted by all the mood music culture plays to practice infidelity by.

If Salzman's assessment of his clinical experience is correct, then it is more important than ever to preach the Gospel message to others. Perhaps Christians need a few words of encouragement that they are on the right track when they continue, under the guidance of the Spirit, to believe and trust and suffer through things with each other. Our greatest infidelity is our faithlessness to the world when we lose confidence in the saving power of the Gospel and the values which it offers still to men.

HOW TO SURVIVE A BAD DAY

BAD trips, they tell us, come from too much acid, but bad days come from too much of life itself. One may muse on what is so rare as a day in June but there is no such poetry connected with what is so common as bad days all around the calendar. February has a certain charm about it, probably because its brevity automatically insures that it will produce fewer bad days than any other month. No matter how you look at them, or try to avoid them, bad days constitute a rainy season in themselves and everybody gets soaked sooner or later.

Indeed, sometimes it does seem that bad days, when most everything goes wrong, are an external and impersonal force of fate with the power to darken the sun, sour happy dispositions, and to stanch the flow of good news while they loose the floods of bad. They may fall on Monday, but it then really seems more like Monday falls on us. And there is no guarantee that the coming of Friday (as in "Thank God it's Friday") will mean the passing of bad days. They pop up on weekends, holidays or, treacherously enough, during long-planned vacations. We know, of course, that these bad days cannot be some force outside of us, that they only seem that way, and yet it is hard to rid ourselves of the victim-like feeling that surges up when a bad day moves in. That is why men have perennially cursed the fates on the one hand while trying to placate them on the other with rabbits' feet and a wariness for walking under ladders or throwing hats on beds. Superstition and astrology have prospered because bad luck and bad days seem to act on us from the outside.

We know well enough our own internal reactions to bad days. When bad news comes in batches, we can get very discouraged, feel very lonely and isolated, or just feel vaguely and unaccountably "down." And these feelings are hard to shake off, mostly because they are hard even to look at in the first place.

Bad days bring out one of the differences between men and women. When a wife, for instance, has a bad day, she can really feel terrible; she can seem, with tears and all, barely capable of living out the next hour. She pours out all her grief to her husband, underscoring the hopelessness of the situation while he is still trying to hang up his hat. This has the effect of turning the day into a bad one for him. He tries to be understanding and sensitive, to offer support and encouragement. Even as he does this, however, he seems to catch, as though it were an infectious disease, her depression and dismay. In short order, he is thoroughly upset. Then the difference shows up; the woman recovers rapidly, the tears are dried and a spirit of fortitude returns. She soars while her husband remains down in the dumps. She is likely to say to him. "What's bothering you anyway?" and, for some reason or other, he never can explain, or perhaps even understand himself exactly what happened to him. All he knows is that he is suddenly in the middle of a bad day and it is hard to get out.

The truth about bad days, of course, depends on how we cope with the stresses or frustrations of the world in which we live. Some people do not respond very well to frustration. They lapse into restlessness or apathy as their style of handling life when their objectives are, for whatever reason, thwarted. Others turn to daydreams, finding in them a magic world of release from the complex reality of their everyday lives. Still others turn aggressive, taking out their bad days on those around them with snarls and scowls. Some even turn back the clock, handling the frustration of bad days by behavior out of their own earlier days. This regression is evident in kicking inanimate objects, getting sick or by taking one's bat, in some symbolic fashion, and going home.

Familiar as these reactions to bad days may be, they are not very effective; in fact, they tend to make things worse because they just frustrate us more. Kicking things does not make the storm clouds disappear; feigning sickness postpones but does not eliminate confronting the conflicts of the day; withdrawing like a spoiled child may seem a short-term success but it is a long-term failure. The all-time classic treatment for the bad day syndrome is a self-administered dose of self-pity mixed with smoldering indignation at the dirty tricks life plays on us. This does not work very well or for very long either.

Getting high on self-pity is a passive and inadequate way of coping with the depression that almost always creeps in somewhere during a bad day. The first thing a person must do is to make some effort to redeem himself from his troubles, rather than waiting for some deliverance from the outside. A good beginning is to listen to what is really going on inside ourselves. This is, more often than not, the key to why things have suddenly gone wrong for us. When we identify correctly what we are really experiencing, we can trace down its origins and see the whole situation in a more realistic manner. It is frequently a small hurt, one that we do not wish to face or to admit to ourselves, that starts a bad day going. Once it is under way, a bad day seems to gain lots of momentum on its own. That is an added reason for getting back to the basic cause of our discomfort. Once we isolate that, we can, if we are honest enough, prevent it from infecting everything else we do.

This is not an easy thing to do, to face our inner selves and call our problems, some of which make us look rather small even in our own eyes, by their right names. It is nonetheless, the first-line of defense against bad days, because it locates the problem not in some cruel fate, but in our own reactions to the difficulties of life. If we persevere in facing our real selves in these moments, we actually develop our own maturity considerably. Our self-esteem increases as the truth of the picture we have of ourselves increases. We handle frustrations in an adult manner and no longer need to revert to some reaction of our childhood.

It is particularly important for the Christian to keep facing the truth about himself and to grow wiser in managing his bad days. As St. Paul wrote to the Galatians with apparent sensitivity to their bad days, "We must never get tired of doing good because if we don't give up the struggle we shall get our harvest at the proper time." St. Paul really had lots of bad days, and he frequently recounts them for his communities to encourage them to keep on going. You can sense that he knows all about bad days when he says to the Romans, "I cannot understand my own behavior. I fail to carry out the things I want to do, and I find myself doing the very things I hate." And how touching his remarks to the Philippians, where he lets them know how much their concern has helped him: "I have been through my initiation and now I am ready for anything anywhere. . . . There is nothing I cannot master with the help of the One who gives me strength. All the same, it was good of you to share with me in my hardships. . . ."

And so it is for all of us in the human condition. Finding that on bad days we do what we don't want to do, we must realize that we desperately need God's help, and that the support of understanding friends means everything. Every Christian will have his share of bad days, and he must be honest with himself in dealing with them, knowing that, in view of the needs of the world, he cannot give up on doing good. His own bad days make him more understanding of the bad days of others, and more compassionate toward every person struggling to stand fast against the headwinds of life. Bad days help us to see each other as brothers better than most of the bad sermons we have ever heard.

Bad days, believe it or not, can have a good side if we take them as a challenge to see more of the truth about ourselves and to give more of ourselves to the service of others. It helps a lot to be able to laugh at ourselves once in a while, but we probably won't find this easy to do until we achieve a good measure of self-knowledge. Self-knowledge has the marvelous effect of helping us to see ourselves in the right perspective.

One thing is clear: there is no cure for the bad day any more than there is for the common cold. There are only more mature ways to handle them when they arise. Just learning this is a big help in learning how to survive them.

MAN AND HIS DEFENSES

EVERYBODY uses psychological defenses. Even the healthiest person finds them functional at times; little white lies, exaggerations, making ourselves sound better motivated than we are, these are but a few of the maneuvers that the best of human beings find in their repertoire. Indeed, these kinds of defenses reveal all of us in the less than perfect, but quite normal, condition that is human. It is only when the use of defenses becomes the main manner in which a man relates to life that we describe him as unhealthy or neurotic.

When does the average person turn to some form of defensive response in the course of everyday life? Ordinarily it is at a moment when he is caught off guard, or unprepared for some situation, or when he has not fully come to terms with some aspect of his personality. We erect defenses around areas that we are not prepared to share fully with other people, even in such questions as our political affiliation, our interest in sports or the arts, or just the amount of our annual salary. Every man wants to appear intelligent, assured, and in control of himself and his life. When a person is suddenly challenged in some set of circumstances he finds a little defensiveness quite helpful in smoothing over the small gaps of anxiety that pop into focus at such moments. So we say something we really do not mean, or assert a claim that is somewhat invalid, or change the subject to something that takes the heat off for us.

The modern American male is, for example, sometimes uneasy if he fails to have a thoroughgoing interest and knowledge about athletics. A little defensiveness, a measure of contrived enthusiasm, and he passes muster with the rest of the boys about the current sports scene. Or, working it the other way around, he may feel embarrassed by his interest in poetry or the opera, but never admit it to his friends to avoid giving the impression that he takes culture seriously. So too, there are areas that are nobody else's business, such as the size of one's paycheck. A little backing and filling, a grumble about the surtax, and a quick change of subject may be employed instead of a straightforward refusal to answer the question.

We sometimes employ relatively harmless defenses to make ourselves look better than we know, in our heart of hearts, we really are. There is, for example, the slow transformation of the good story we have been telling for years. At first it was something we had heard about; gradually, in the retelling, we eliminate the middle man and tell it as if we had been present; in the final version, we have simplified it to the point that we are no longer the observant reporter but the main character himself. We can get pretty good at this, so good, in fact, that after a period of time we really believe the story ourselves.

All these examples have something in common with all defense mechanisms, even those that are signs of some more serious personal problem. Basically, each of them employs some form of denial or disguise of the truth. They all varnish reality a little, and toward the same end, to give a better picture of ourselves. And we use them, in milder situations, for exactly the same reason that more disturbed people do: to hold ourselves together and even to inhance ourselves in moments of uneasiness. We get defensive, in other words, whenever our picture of ourselves is under threat because some of our actions or feelings do not really fit in with this picture. Defenses arise when inconsistencies begin to show through at some level of our consciousness. These inconsistencies make us anxious and the defenses have the very functional effect of toning down our anxiety. We bridge our normal inconsistencies with defensive statements or behavior because it is much easier to do this than it is to re-examine and possibly change the picture we have of ourselves.

For example, the man who has an idea of himself as always in control of his feelings is quite threatened by a sudden impulse of anger. It just doesn't fit the way he has identified himself. The strong feeling really challenges his supposedly secure self-knowledge. But there is the anger and something has to be done about it. When we are surprised by such a contradictory feeling, the first impulse is to deny it, precisely because of its inconsistency in our lives. "No, I'm not angry!" a man will say, erecting a first line of defense against this intrusive feeling. The strange thing, of course, is that he may say this in such a clearly defensive tone of voice that he actually reveals his anger to the other person anyhow. But that is not the point here; the defenses serve him, his own inner world, his cherished picture of himself. He has denied his anger in order to put it out of the way for himself. This is obviously not a very good long-term strategy but it may be very effective for the moment. This is exactly where defenses are of some use to the healthy person. They give him time to think, they remove the pressure of the instant, and they may make it possible for him to take a fresh look at himself once the initial sense of threat has tapered off a bit.

I am suggesting that the genuine ideal which we have of being completely open and defenseless in all our relationships is probably a little unrealistic even for the healthy and sincere human being. Because he is not perfect, because self-discovery is an ongoing process, and because defenses are not always terribly bad things, the ordinary person should not be too disappointed to find vestiges of defensive behavior in his life. He may quite gradually be able to eliminate a great deal of it, but he should not necessarily feel that he is unhealthy because he cannot do this all at once. In fact, some people who demand an instant and total openness from others—and this is all the rage in certain settings these days—may be more unhealthy than the individuals who find themselves somewhat less than ready to bare their innermost secrets with complete candor.

Growth in openness occurs through time, in the only way that any growth process takes place. Some form of defense is probably necessary for the average Christian wayfarer while he is struggling to understand himself fully enough to be more completely open to his fellow men. We have to respect this truth, both in ourselves and in our friends, and not rudely tear down, from the outside, defensive structures that can only be given up, in the long run, from within.

REACTION-FORMATION

AT times man seems like a self-sealing tire: as soon as something punctures his inflated picture of himself he quickly patches the hole with the psychological cement of his defenses. He can then keep going without examining himself carefully because he has managed to keep his self-esteem intact. Reaction-formation, despite its clinically formidable sound, is one of man's most effective ways of defending himself against what is really going on inside himself.

Reaction-formation describes that process by which we can disquise our true motives or desires when these would cause us guilt or shame if we really faced up to them. The defense consists in strongly expressing the very opposite of what we are in truth experiencing. For example, a person will become anxious when he feels a strong attraction for some activity that clashes with what he thinks he should feel. He may feel anger toward his wife or children but this is quite incompatible with his image of himself as a loving husband and father. Reaction-formation expresses itself in an over-concern and an excessive solicitude for their welfare. He is, in other words, proving to himself that he does not feel the way he really does. He reassures himself by stifling these contrary impulses through an unbalanced show of affection and attention.

It works the same way with other sets of impulses. The person strongly attracted to erotic material may defend himself by vigorous attack on all such material. The many who wonder whether he is really as manly as he would like to be may throw himself into a spate of supposedly brawny activities. The person who is drawn to read forbidden books may block this impulse through leading a crusade against such literature. The inwardly violent individual may become the ardent champion of law and order. In all these, however, it is not the external world the person is trying to reorder; it is rather the inner world of his own personality.

The biggest clue to the presence of reaction-formation is the fact that it manifests itself in an excessive manner. The individual employing this defense does indeed "protest too much" as he strives to handle his own emotional conflicts through opposite words and deeds. He goes just a little too far in asserting his righteousness, his probity, or his manliness. It is not too difficult to spot this kind of behavior in others. We all recognize someone who comes on too strong. It is much more difficult to identify it in ourselves, since the mechanism operates at a level below our own consciousness. Whenever we find ourselves pushing something beyond the way normal, healthy persons react we have a sign to which we should pay attention.

The saddest part of the consistent use of self-deceptive reaction-formation is the toll it takes of others. Parents who overprotect their children to comfort their own uneasiness often leave the children really unprotected to face the rigors of life. When the child gets hurt or in trouble, the defensive parent can point to the excessive evidence of concern and say, "How could this happen? Look at everything that I have done for you!" So too, the overzealous reformer often ends up deforming the lives of other people but comforts himself by saying, "I was only trying to do the Lord's work." The overenthusiastic censor destroys humanity's opportunities for truth and wisdom as he makes a funeral pyre of the books he secretly wants to read.

It is clear that not every reformer, nor everyone concerned with good works or good taste, is a victim of fooling himself because of his own distorted fascination. The sign of this defense in operation is always the overdone quality of the individual's activities. He insists just too much and this becomes obvious to others even when he cannot understand it himself.

Healthy people are able to face the whole range of their impulses and to look beneath them for an understanding of them. This is a challenge but not a dismaying one. We should never be surprised by any of our feelings. We should only be upset if we do not have the courage to face them, call them by their correct names, and try to understand why they have come into being. That is the way of the undefensive man who cares more about the truth than about kidding himself about life.

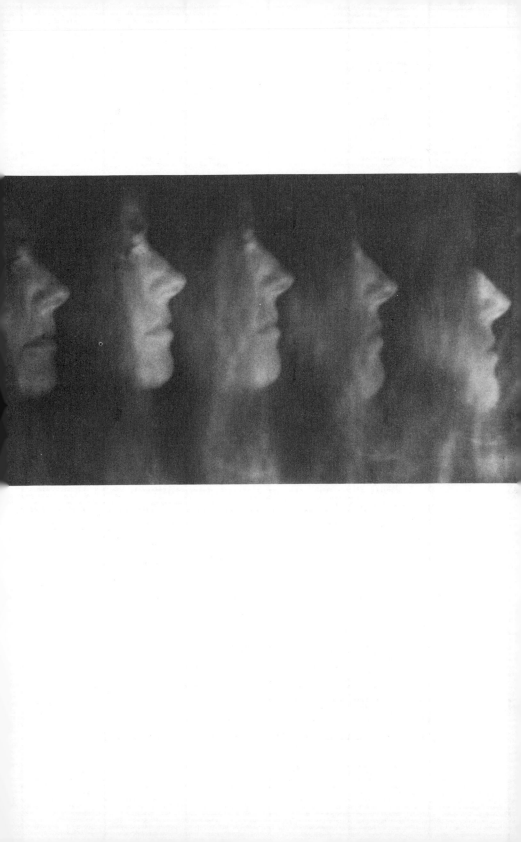

PROJECTION

PROJECTION is one of the defenses dearest to the hypocrites of history. Christ himself described it perfectly and most of us can recognize it instantly. It has had a long and hardy life because it does such wonderful things for the people who employ it. Projection enables us to look away from our bad points by transferring them to people around us. We need not, therefore, indict ourselves because we can condemn the fault in our neighbor. We literally project our bad points, like a personal underground movie of our own personality, into the world around us. It is then safe to be judgmental about the problem because our irritation can be directed away from ourselves and onto others.

For example, if a person has a tendency to be insensitive and aggressive in dealing with others, he would be very uncomfortable if he acknowledged this truth to himself. It would challenge his carefully guarded image of himself. Projection becomes the defense of choice because it enables him to see and criticize this tendency in others. He clearly handles his own problem in a very roundabout manner but he also protects himself from the truth that would upset him if he had to face it. This individual deals with his own flaws by seeing them in others and by attacking his own problem in them. His anger at others is not based on his own bad quality and he is only giving them what they deserve.

Projection is very widely used precisely because it works so smoothly and seems so logical and reasonable. That, of course, is what goes into making a good defense mechanism. In this case it is literally true that the best defense is a good offense. The clue to the use of projection is two-fold. First of all, the individual seems to find his own problem in practically everybody else in the world. Everyone cheats, is dishonorable, is lazy or a liar. The person who uses projection comes up with the same diagnosis in too many cases. This is a measure of the severity of his own problem. The second telling characteristic of those who employ this defense is their attribution of the bad quality in an exaggerated way to other people.

The best person for us to examine for projection is ourself. It is interesting to note how easily we can find projection in other people; why, such a thing could never be true of us! And yet this is a common if very subtle use of projection itself. Because it takes the heat off ourselves, we turn almost instinctively to it for protection. This illustrates another quality of all the defense mechanisms: we do not consciously choose to use them. If we acknowledged what we were doing, we could not fool ourselves and the defenses would not be effective.

That is why for many centuries spiritual writers have suggested deep self-examination as an indispensable part of the necessary quest for self-knowledge. Although they never have used the term "defense mechanism" they have been clearly aware of the way defenses operate in the human personality. With the wisdom of their observations and experience they have suggested that what irritates us most about other people is probably the fault that we ourselves possess. That is projection in action, and with their sensitivity to it, many spiritual writers exhibit the insight that has made their work endure.

It was projection that Christ contrasted to the meaning of integrity and honesty: "Why do you observe the splinter in your brother's eye and never notice the plank in your own? How can you say to your brother, 'Brother, let me take out the splinter that is in your eye,' when you cannot see the plank in your own? Hypocrite! Take the plank out of your own eye first, and then you will see clearly enough to take out the splinter that is in your brother's eye."

PERFECTIONISM

THE desire to do things perfectly has always seemed praise-worthy enough, so praiseworthy, indeed, that some people are sur-prised to discover that it is often used as a defense mechanism. Perfectionism has had a long and fabled history as a psychological defense. In principle, perfectionism works like the rest of the de-fenses; when something slips into the edge of our awareness that doesn't fit the picture we have of ourselves we automatically set up a barrier of denial or disguise against it in order to keep up our good opinion of ourselves. Defenses turn away, at least tempo-rarily, the anxiety we would feel if we took a long hard look at what was really going on inside ourselves.

So it is with perfectionism. When we are unconsciously uneasy about doing something, even when it is an important thing to get done, we invoke the mechanism of perfectionism. We hold on to whatever it is—the book we are writing, the decision we are sup-posed to make, the opinion we are asked to form—telling our-selves and others that we haven't got it quite right yet, that it needs a few added touches, or that the times aren't right, or that we need more information. However we describe it, we are play-ing the perfectionism game, the time-buying device that protects us from the possibility of conflict of criticism. The person caught up in the perfectionism routine never gets anything finished be-cause he never gets anything quite right; it is actually easier on his ego to postpone things than to take the risk of making some kind of mistake or allowing the world to see that he is fallible after all. I remember a colleague in graduate school who worked for years on a plan for a doctoral thesis, seeking a holy grail kind of perfec-tion in his research that would make it unique and immune from criticism. The fear of not covering every possibility, the anxiety over taking any risk at all paralyzed him. The years wasted away and the thesis was never written. He lost in a certain way, but in the inner world of his own personality he kept on winning. He used the defense of perfectionism with the skill of a field marshall. He never did have to take a chance and he never was criticized, but he missed the doctorate and the chance to grow at the same time.

The examples of perfectionism in action are not hard to find. In what we call (or used to call) scrupulosity, for example, the person was always too preoccupied with saying his prayers right that he never got them finished. His religious life was confined to a very small area of constant concern and he never had to look beyond this. There is something dissociative about this kind of defense, a breaking off of some thought or action from the feeling that should go with it. Through perfectionism, like stepping on all the cracks in the sidewalk or repeating some prayers endlessly, a person holds back a tide of worry that would otherwise engulf him. That is why these devices, simple though they may seem, are of such significance to those who use them. These people are trying to solve the problem of life through their little rituals, holding the hounds of life at bay with their defensive tactic. Obviously, when a person gets this defensive, he needs psychological help.

Perfectionism, however, is also found among people who seem like they have something of value to contribute to the world. They hold back out of fear, waiting for fairer weather, or until added years or some other event makes it safe for them to write their book, make their decision, or even get married. They want to wait until they are able to do it perfectly, and that, of course, is a very long and self-defeating wait.

Fear is the enemy of most of our growth, and perfectionism is not an easy defense for the fearful to put aside. A first step, however, is the realization that the defense is very crippling and, in the long run, one that shuts a person out from life and from other people. It also keeps a person from ever tapping his own resources fully and freely or from the liberating discovery that the Christian life is designed for imperfect people. And that is a discovery that no fear should make us postpone, for *now* is the acceptable time, now is the time of salvation.

RATIONALIZATION

RATIONALIZATION is probably the most common type of defense mechanism. We all use it, or are tempted to use it, almost every day. When we employ a rationalization we reflect our deep need to keep our behavior at least apparently consistent. We want our actions and thoughts to hang together in one piece with our feelings. We desire to appear in our own eyes and in the eyes of others as logical and reasonable persons, whose behavior is not random or disjointed but integrated and unified. By its very name, rationalization suggests the defensive maneuvers by which our actions are made to seem rational, that is to say, reasonable and sensibly motivated.

A famous psychological experiment offers a good example. Under hypnosis an individual is told that, although he will not recall this suggestion, he will go over and open a window when the experimenter takes a handkerchief out of his pocket. The subject is brought out of the trance and all seems as it was before. After a few moments the signal is given as the experimenter removes his handkerchief. When the individual who has been hypnotized moves toward the window, his motivation for doing so is not at all clear to him. But there he is at the window, ready to throw it open for no good reason. It is a piece of behavior which he must make rational to himself and to the others in the room. He looks around, says, "It's a little stuffy in here," and opens the window.

What has taken place? The person has been moved to this action by hypnotic suggestion; he consciously does not know why he is doing what he proposes to do. He must, then, make this activity of opening the window fit in with the rest of his behavior. The remark about the need for fresh air is a convenient if not carefully planned rationalization. It is, in other words, something that he does without really understanding it; the rationalization is a socially acceptable statement and it makes him appear intelligent and logically motivated as he carries out the hypnotist's suggestion. He has given a good reason for his action. His behavior seems to hold together. The only difficulty, of course, is that it is not the real reason for his opening the window.

The dynamics of every rationalization are quite similar. When we do not or cannot face the real reasons for what we do, we can easily produce explanations which meet the usual criteria for defense mechanisms: they are self-enhancing, not necessarily conscious, and they either deny or disguise the real truth. The essence of the rationalization lies precisely in giving a good, cogent reason for what we do or say. It protects us from facing the anxiety that would arise if we allowed ourselves to face directly the inconsistency that is really present in many of our actions. Rationalization, in the long run, fools only the rationalizer. It makes him feel as if he were a logical and reasonable person even if it does not convince anybody else.

The danger in defensive adjustment lies in the effects of regular doses of self-deception. We get hung-up, like drug addicts, on our defenses, and the person harmed is really our own self. This is true when defenses are employed extensively to cope with life. We can get caught in our own web of explanations and lose sight of the truth about ourselves altogether. The sad part is that we often do not fool others for very long. The habitual rationalizer is quickly recognized by others. Our language has many nicknames, such as "Alibi Ike," which are applied to persons who always have an excuse or a lengthy explanation but hardly ever the truth about their own motivation.

Aside from the custom-tailored rationalizations which we fashion to meet our own measurements, American Culture provides a whole rack of them ready to wear. There are countless variations to drape inconsistent moral behavior, most of them based on over-simplifications of so-called situation ethics. There is the ancient adage that "Everybody does it" to make grafting and cheating more digestible. There is probably nothing more pathetically defensive than the starlet's explanation that she performs in the nude when it "is an integral part of the plot and it is done tastefully." Exhibitionism, by any other name, hardly merits the badge of maturity. So too, the film-goer looking for some erotic thrills finds his self-esteem enhanced when he can think of himself as a liberated and discriminating buff of the art film. A man on his fifth luncheon martini can even quote St. Paul about a little wine being good for the stomach.

All these defenses cover up what is really going on inside ourselves. Rationalization is the enemy of wholeness because it prevents us from really seeing ourselves as we are. It covers up our lack of growth and keeps us from truly coming to terms with our real personalities. Many self-styled "free" people are prisoners of the unresolved problems against which their illlusory life-style is the chief defense. There is hardly a rationalization more tempting than the one that makes us more knowledgeable and sophisticated than the rest of man.

When a person gets mesmerized by his own rationalizations, he usually gets progresssively more defensive in trying to maintain his self-esteem. Increased defensiveness, a rejection of all criticism, a stubborn insistence on one's own explanatory tales—these are the signs of a person who is in serious trouble because of his lack of ability to face the truth about himself. It is always his wife's fault, or his boss's incompetence; or it is the fault of authority if we are underlings and the fault of underlings if we are in authority. Desperately, the neurotically defensive person keeps patching up the fabric of his self-created world. In it, he is always the good guy, the misunderstood hero, the victim of a systematically capricious fate.

Most of us, when we reflect on defense mechanisms, get a little defensive ourselves. We start by applying the yardstick of defensive behavior to somebody other than ourselves. We say, "I wish so and so would read that," or "That's just the trouble with my husband," or, "So that's why my pastor is the way he is." These are remarkably defensive applications. They shield us from examining ourselves and our own willingness to face the truth while they give us the mildly exquisite joy of being able to hang a label on somebody outside ourselves.

We may, of course, be quite right in applying these reflections to others, but, if we exempt ourselves from self-examination, we may also have a clue that we are not quite as open as we like to think. A man does not have to beat himself to the ground with self-analysis, but even the healthiest of us might look first at ourselves to see if we really tell ourselves the truth about what we do or say. Like charity, measuring the depth of defensiveness begins at home.

LONGING

EVERY person knows the experience of longing. Men long for many things in a lifetime and, no matter what they acquire or achieve, the ache of longing is never completely eased. It is a sign of man's continuing incompleteness; he cannot hold his most wondrous moments in focus for long; he cannot trap time nor stay change, the elements that eat away at every life; he moves or is moved relentlessly forward, always searching but never quite finding enough to fill him.

Rachel yearned for her children who were no more, and Christ longed for the people of Jerusalem who would not hear him as he wept over that city. In every age men have longed for other goals: wealth through alchemy, an earthly paradise through voyages of discovery, and, in our own time, contentment through affluence. Men have only yearned more deeply as they have faced the disillusion of getting what they thought they wanted, or the disappointment of grasping at the mirages that dot the journey of life. It is never quite all there and so man feels that he is never quite all there either. There is always a new challenge, a constant eroding of achieved securities, always a sign of our capacity for fulfillment and our failure to find the right formula for it.

Man has abundant evidence of his incompleteness, of his openness to being filled, and the impossibility of his ever being completely fulfilled in this world. So St. Paul could write of the cosmic longing in which we all have a share. "From the beginning till now the entire creation, as we know, has been groaning in one great act of giving birth; and not only creation, but all of us who possess the first fruits of the Spirit, we, too, groan inwardly as we wait for our bodies to be set free" (Romans 8:22, 23). This is the restlessness of the heart of which St. Augustine wrote, the restlessness that is quieted only by God himself. Our longing is one of the "rumors of angels" which sociologist Peter Berger recently described, a hint of the fulfilling God who lives beyond all our longing and who alone can respond to it.

This does not mean that man cannot experience God's faithful response to his deepest longings in this world. Indeed, Christ promised life, "life to the full," to those who followed him. Our longing points to the level of experience in this life where the Spirit touches us and puts us in contact with the source of all life. This is the level of our relationships with each other and it is deep beneath the surface at which so many of man's contemporary longings are pursued. Indeed, a man cannot even experience the real meaning of longing unless he gets inside life and begins to understand what it means to believe in and trust others and to find his selfishness shattered by the challenge of hoping and loving.

The saddest part of man's present plight is that he grasps at the shadows of superficial values in his quest for fulfillment. His deepest longings, however, transcend the latest styles in clothes and automobiles. They reveal the emptiness of his current search for an erotic nirvana and the utter loneliness at the top that follows upon men's aggressive hunt for power. These goals do not match the full dimensions of man's nature and so they multiply rather than relieve his longing. A pathetic footnote to this is the news that *Playboy* will not accept any advertising that makes men aware of their shortcomings. No ads spotlighting his frailty or his incomplete education can find a place in its pages because this might break the spell of sophistication and contentment that the magazine supposedly has conferred upon him.

Only real-life experience in seeking to love others responsibly brings man to an understanding of himself and the kinds of values for which he truly yearns, no matter how disguised his gropings may be. At the level of faith, hope and love man knows his greatest longing and can receive his most fulfilling response. It is also, of course, where he knows his most painful disappointments. Believing, hoping, and loving bring him to life but they also make him vulnerable in a way that he can never be if he shields himself from these experiences. Because authentic living can be so painful many people back away from it. Seeking to avoid hurt, they merely intensify their longing. Less important goals can be substituted readily but at the dangerously high price that these people may never know what life is all about.

A husband, for example, can replace his marriage with his job. He protects himself from facing the demands of loving his wife and children by plunging into work so that it keeps him at a defensive distance from them. So, too, a wife can find many distractions to fill her calendar but these leave the core of her life quite empty and unexplored. Any of us can do this in a culture that proposes so many pleasurable distractions that they prevent us from ever knowing who we are, and keep us from testing ourselves in the trusting and loving that give life its meaning.

It is the paradox of Christianity that it has always pointed to the only situations in life where longing can be overcome and that these situations are the most dangerous ones for man to enter. The paradox is heightened by the fact that life is given to others and attained by ourselves only when we are prepared to face pain and a special kind of dying. There is a crucifixion in responsibly loving other persons, an invitation to death that is also an invitation to resurrection. We find life when we are ready to lose ourselves for the sake of others in the process. Longing for life and love is a signal that man's fate is worked out in the dynamics of being ready to die to himself in order to find himself. That is how it works, and the only way it works. But selfishness and being ready to die are hardly popular commodities at the present moment; our flight toward fulfillment is in another direction altogether. It is an illusion as old as alchemy.

The worst danger of our present civilization is in the ease with which it provides escape from life, the way it can exempt us from facing the real issues of our identity as human beings. Man has manufactured countless wonders and a thousand distractions which bring him no closer to an understanding of himself. Self-understanding follows a painful path and there are progressively fewer who are willing to take it. The strange thing is the reverse paradox that is provided by this. The more man can have of the goods of life, the less he is able to deal with the riches of his own personality and the more he is estranged from self-understanding. The more he wants to avoid death out of fear, the less able he is to taste life. But longing, somewhere deep down where the sparks of his humanity are still fiery bright, he will be restless and wonder why. Innoculated against the deepest feelings of his nature, he will long for them all the more. The cost of living becomes too high, but the price of longing rises higher still. So Archibald MacLeish could write:

The crime against life, the worst of all crimes, is not to feel. And there was never, perhaps, a civilization in which that crime, the crime of torpor, of lethargy, of apathy, the snake-like sin of cold-ness-at-the-heart was commoner than in our technological civilization in which the emotionless emotions of adolescent boys are mass produced on television screens to do our feeling for us, and woman's longing for her life is twisted, by singing commercials, into a longing for a new detergent, family-sized, which will keep her hands as innocent as though she had never lived. It is the modern painless death, this commercialized atrophy of the heart. None of us is safe from it.

Longing remains a significant clue about us. It is not something to be smothered, or disguised. It reveals the depths of our nature and points to the equally deep level of experience which constitutes the ground of life. For the Christian, it resonates with the Gospel, gives meaning to hope, dares us to die for a fuller life, and opens us to the Spirit who gives us life and life to the full.

HOW CAN I TELL
WHEN I NEED HELP?

ONLY a very grim and unredeemed theology tells man that he must suffer alone. Nobody who tries to understand the gospels can possibly believe or live by this notion. Life is filled with more than enough loneliness; it is harsh and stoic to think that one must not admit, talk about, or share one's pain with others. Stiff upper lips are fine, and biting the bullet is great in old movies about the British in India, but turning one's tears to a wall of loneliness is both unnecessary and unchristian in a world where, according to the apostle Paul, we are meant to help bear one another's burdens. The Christian community, now that we have shed the analogies of monarchies and armies, is the place where a person never again has to be alone with his sorrows.

However, the trouble is that we have put a lot of emphasis in recent years on learning how to listen to others when they are in trouble or in pain. This is a good idea, but where does it leave me when I want to talk, when, in other words, I need somebody to listen to me? It is right here that a lot of people get hung-up because, although they know they are supposed to listen to others, they don't or won't let themselves enjoy the same simple privilege. They are still driven by the forces that say they are not worthy of taking another's time, or they are ashamed of the weakness they would thereby reveal. To use an old-fashioned but valid idea, they may be too proud to let others have a look at their human flaws.

"Don't keep it all in" another old phrase of advice goes, but that is exactly what many people, faces strained like those of Olympic runners, attempt to do. That strategy has little chance of success. Nothing that is pushed down inside us stays down there very long; the roots, like those of a weeping willow seeking water, multiply themselves in the dark, heaving up a part of personality here and cracking another dimension of it there. The man who hides his pain even from himself only creates a new and disguised set of pains. Lots of soured stomachs, faulted hearts and, of course, bad tempers are the result of emotional problems that have not been dealt with directly. Man keeps trying to make his problems clear; when he does not let himself do it straightforwardly he does it symbolically. But emotional pains never just go away.

The best thing a man with a burden can do is to follow St. Paul's advice. He should let somebody else shoulder the weight with him for a while. That, of course, does not mean that he lets the other person carry the whole burden; it suggests rather the simplest and best medicine there is for a person under emotional pressure—that he make an effort to share this strain with another person, to end his loneliness and shatter the bonds of inner suppression by telling at least some of it to somebody else. When we talk about "getting help" we cover a great range of human experiences. It can mean seeing a professional person, a psychiatrist or a psychologist for example; it can mean talking to your wife or your best friend or, sometimes, your bartender; it can mean, in one of the constant mysteries of life, taking the terrible risk of talking to a stranger, someone whose only bond with you is the human condition. Whenever we try to talk honestly, it is almost sure to be a help to us. We don't even have to do it well. Many have experienced the redeeming understanding of another when all they could do was sob out their problem in a disconnected and disjointed way. It makes no difference; the essential part is that, for whatever reason, we have stopped standing all by ourselves.

Yes, but when are we just being a burden to others, bothering them when they have enough troubles of their own? When, a man can rightfully ask, can I tell that I need the help of another? There are a few rules of thumb we might follow in this regard, although we need never be afraid of what true understanding from another may do to us. A person should get help if it is clear that something is gnawing at him and that he is not dealing with it directly. When a man does not sleep well, when his dreams will not let him rest and he begins to wake long before the first light—these are clear signs of an unresolved difficulty that the person is not handling well on his own. A feeling of being depressed that just won't lift away from a man's soul the way it usually does, a sudden and chronic failure of self-confidence that makes a man afraid to try the things he knows he can do—these are big signs too. When a man finds that he cannot get down to work over a protracted period of time, when he gets lots of rest and still feels tired, when he begins to drink to drown things out—all of these indicate that the individual should get some outside help.

At times the signs that a person needs assistance are far more subtle. He may only catch them in the reactions of those with whom he works, or from the truth, if he lets himself look at it, that he seems always to be getting into disagreements and that there is a certain pattern to them in which he ends up justifying himself. These give reasons enough to talk to somebody else rather than plowing ahead as though these behaviors were of no account. Then, of course, there are the ordinary garden variety pains of life, the things we should really talk about to somebody else before we feel so sorry for ourselves that we permanently distort the experience in the cramped dimension of our solitary world.

One thing is certain: we are more likely to harm ourselves by neglecting to seek help than we are by attempting to reach another with our problem. The greatest harm, the thing that exiles us permanently in our loneliness, comes from waiting too long, from making excuses, or from being unwilling to let others see a part of our own painful truth. You can tell you need to get some help when you sense that unmistakable inner urge to get something that hurts into words, when you long to talk to somebody about your own life. That is the time to move out and take the risk of sharing your doubts and fears with another. It is also a moment of redemption and reaffirmation, and we can use all of those we can get. But we rarely get them alone.

I THINK YOU'LL RECOGNIZE HIM . . .

. . . WHEN you see him. Or maybe I should say hear him because he talks a lot. I refer to your good friend—but only in a manner of speaking—the man who won't let you agree with him. You have met him before, you say? And you have come away a little bewildered, I am sure. Perhaps he is the kind of person Thomas à Kempis kept meeting when he went innocently abroad in the world, the kind who he said, in his famous *Imitation of Christ*, caused him to return home less a man. That is about how you feel after a chat with a person who just will not let you get on common ground with him. It is like an evening on a merry-go-round, plucking in the darkness for the elusive brass ring of relationship.

The man who will not let you agree with him is not exactly a man of principle. He moves from one side of a question to another, not because he believes in something so firmly, but because he wants to stay on the opposite side from you. He is not much help in running a business, or building a friendship; he is absolutely deadly for collegiality. He is, however, to be found everywhere. Being alert to him is one of the few defenses against him, but there is really no foolproof response.

This fellow seems affable enough. That is why it defies reason to watch him operate. He maneuvers away from you at a critical point in your conversation, the moment, as a matter of fact, when you get just a little too close to him. The reason he will not let you agree with him is because he does not want you on the inside of his life. He does not want anybody there and, over the years, he has developed a sure technique for saving his soul for himself. It takes a lot of energy and a willingness to bear hearing himself being inconsistent, but this individual allows this inconsistency without so much as an embarrassed blush. For him the important thing is to keep you from thinking you have a hold on him; in his own view, he pictures himself as maintaining his independence. It is a sad and fruitless deception, but when he wakes up lonely some morning he will blame the rest of men rather than himself.

When you meet one of these people, do not make the mistake of trying to win him over. You just frighten him more and increase his defensiveness when you do that. It is a natural impulse, however, to be friendly and open and we are hurt ourselves when an honest attempt on our part is met with a quick snap of the conversation cape that sends us sprawling on our faces.

It is best, I think, to let these people alone. Put the burden on them. If they want to be disagreeable, then it will have to be for their own reasons, not for ones that we supply for them. This is the psychological equivalent to the old biblical saying about pouring coals of fire on the head of an opponent. It is also the way to be wise as serpents and guileless as doves. It saves you energy, passes the frustration on to him, and keeps him from impeding whatever you are trying to get done. That may sound a little mean but it is a good example of Christian practicality. You help the man who won't let you agree with him most by not playing his game, by not handing him the shells he will promptly fire back at you. After he fails often enough, he may begin to question himself and to restyle his relationships with others. So watch out for this man who gets through life by not letting others agree with him. And as a favor to him, don't take him out to lunch this week.

IT LOOKS SO DIFFERENT FROM HERE

ONE of the most common and yet most difficult of life's experiences requires us to re-examine our past and to redefine it according to a more adult perspective. This is a hard thing to do because we all put a filter, usually a rosy-hued one, on our memories. That is no news to any of us; our remembrance of things past is sweetened by the passage of time so that all the bad guys and the embarrassing incidents are in the background, out of focus now, like the extras in a movie. That is why nostalgia turns our hearts warm with longing for those good times, when we had real heroes, a reliable faith, good old-fashioned winters, and the promise of true love. Those things seem so hard to get now, harder by far than the rationed items of World War II. Perhaps that is why, at a generation's distance, they look so appealing.

Because of the enchantment generated by distance we find it painful to look deeply into the past and to awaken memories and relationships that we would rather leave undisturbed. Yet this is a necessary feature of growing up, an essential task for anybody who wants to live honestly in the present. Perhaps the most challenging thing any person must redefine as he gets older is his own homelife. We would all like to remember it as perfect, but a glorified memory would be a distortion for all of us, because no family is perfect and none ever will be. As a matter of fact, no healthy thing is perfect. When we forget this basic truth of life we get in trouble. And so, human beings thrive in environments that are healthy rather than perfect. If we suffer from a need to see the past as perfect, maybe something unhealthy is there (just a little something anyway) that we do not really want to look at even though it is a part of our history and therefore a part of ourselves.

Probably the most sensitive area regarding our homelife centers on our feelings towards our parents. We don't like to say negative things about them no matter how human they are; lots of brawls are still triggered by those hostile insults about our forebears. That we choose to attack on that level shows the significance and the sensitivity of this area for everybody. But, when you are maturing, you can give up the idea that your parents are perfect without diminishing them in any way. You can admit their humanity without resenting them for it and without feeling shortchanged or disillusioned by life. Only the very fearful have to hold onto a childhood view which sees their parents as great magical figures filling the sky and doing no wrong. These people never want to face the truth about themselves either, and life becomes a child's garden of verses, full of sunlight and statues, but not a place in which real people can live.

The time comes for everyone to put himself and his past into better perspective. It is important to be able to separate ourselves enough from the past to see it as it actually was, and thus better understand ourselves as we are. The need to see things realistically is not a call for debunking the past or blaming our parents for everything we manage to do wrong ourselves. We need not be cynically self-indulgent, as Oscar Wilde was when he wrote that "children begin by loving their parents; as they grow older they judge them; sometimes they forgive them." As mature Christians we can see farther than that. We know that a more realistic view of our parents has a redemptive quality to it; we thereby free them from our own unreasonable demands that they be absolutely flawless. To see them more realistically may be to draw closer to them humanly, and to sense and possess what they have truly given to us so that we might hand it on to others.

UNOBTRUSIVE MEASURES

MAN loves to look at himself and to learn, especially from the moments when he is off guard, what he is really like. That is why programs like "Candid Camera" have been popular, and why sitting quietly and watching the parade of life go by is as much fun as going to the movies. It is only when we become self-conscious —getting ourselves arranged for a photograph or a home movie— that we obscure our true selves. Why is it that we are always so surprised when the picture really captures the character of the one photographed? Is he or she that much different in everyday life? Most of us, especially when we are looking at pictures of ourselves, seem to think so. There is not much *vérité* in the *cinema* of our own experience.

There is, however, a good way to get a look at ourselves if we are really interested in some subtle but truthful self-revelations. Truth might not necessarily be what we are after; some of us do prefer those gauzy photos in which our wrinkles and blemishes are airbrushed away. But, if we have the heart for it, we can look at the trail we leave behind us and find it strewn with tiny revelations about ourselves. Psychologists speak of certain measures of human behavior as "unobtrusive." That is to say, they are not deliberately set up as personal measurements in the way questionnaires and psychological tests are; they just pop up out of our daily rounds. They are the results of our own activities, the outcome of our own choices, and, when they are properly illumined, they project a sharply defined profile of ourselves. Unobtrusive measures, like our fingerprints, are all around us, providing us with quite reliable self-knowledge.

For example, the number of cigarette stubs in an ash tray tells us something if we care to read the sign for ourselves; it is particularly informative if we have been comforting ourselves with some rationalization that we have actually cut down on smoking. Some could learn a lot from a good look at their liquor bill. These measures are rather obvious, of course, and they probably do not apply to very many readers. But how about the way you read the newspaper or magazine? What is the section you read first, or perhaps what is the only section you read? And what exactly does that say about you? And then there are those bitten down fingernails, and you keep saying that you are not really anxious about anything. How many sleeping pills or tranquilizers are left in that medicine cabinet? And how high is that pile of unanswered mail? Do you really believe it when you say that you know where everything is on that desk? And what is behind those subjects that you would rather not talk about? Listen carefully to yourself the next time you think that you are unobtrusively changing the subject of an upsetting conversation.

If I go much further with this, I'm afraid I'll get depressed myself. But self-knowledge should not really be something that gets us down. It may take a little courage to look at these things, but they are the very things that give us a better understanding of ourselves. These unobtrusive measures may, in some way or other, be faint but reliable signals about the way we relate to other people. They can, if we allow them, be clues that alert us to why things go wrong, or why misunderstandings arise. They may even point to a way to do something about them by doing something about ourselves. Naturally, we don't want to get so absorbed in counting these things that we forget everything else. Perhaps it is best to be unobtrusive in measuring our own unobtrusive measures, to couple forgiveness with perception about our faults. If we do that, we can only be wiser and happier for it.

THE MODERN SOURCES OF
FAITH, HOPE AND LOVE

FAITH, hope and love, according to St. Paul, are "the things that last," the values that never wear out in the lives of persons who make an honest effort to live by the Spirit. Faith, hope and love are profound words, symbols that serve us well in capturing the meaning of our most significant experiences with each other. These words which express such a great share of mankind's living experience should not be used lightly.

But faith, hope and love are currently for sale cheap in various contemporary markets. These values, now hollowed out and insubstantial, are sold to an unsuspecting world that longs for something better and cannot understand its disappointment when it must settle for something so much less than the original meaning of these concepts. A great automobile manufacturer, for example, markets the faith that people would like to find again by saying that its make of car offers you "something to believe in." But faith in cars that are designed to wear out in a few years does not nourish a man through a lifetime. It can only deceive him, cheapening the idea of believing in anything. Using a big word for a small meaning and playing on human longings in such a way as this is an insult to the real meaning of man.

And hope now comes from horoscopes, the astrologers playing sleight of hand with the stars in order to sustain people through the difficulties and decisions of life. But Aquarian hope is as cold as starlight as it weaves a spell of wishful thinking around man, inviting him to trust his future to a fate outside of himself. Hope through astrology makes man passive and insignificant, a plaything of the gods, whose dignity is only diminished by linking him to the blind forces of the zodiac.

And no matter what anybody tells you, love comes easy these days. And how else but by way of marijuana, that sweet smell in the air that generates a feeling of community and makes you a first class citizen of the Woodstock nation? Marijuana gives you good vibrations, smoothing over all the conflicts and differences that seem to emerge in everyday life, and making love something that is readily available, part of the better living through chemistry that appeals to so many people these days. But to use the word love as if it meant nothing more than warm feelings is to indulge in a fatal sentimentality that only tricks and betrays the innocent. It is hardly any wonder people can look at these easy varieties of faith, hope and love, and ask, "Is that all there is?"

Traditional values are debased by the shabby use of the words which have only slowly come into our language to describe them. As psychologist Sigmund Koch has pointed out, the words for our most important experiences have not gotten into the language easily. Each verbal symbol has a long history just as each one has been tested by successive generations. The richest connotations of human encounters have only gradually been compressed into words like faith, hope, and love. When a man uses them, he can do so either as one who has entered deeply into the human experiences which they signify so that they reflect his own depth or he can speak them so that they sound false to the ear, because he utters them with no real sense of their significance at all. We live in an age in which many of our most sacred word symbols are used by those who have never entered the depths of human experience at all. The result is a confusing kind of superficiality which takes away the majesty and the meaning of man's human vocabulary and does his nature a great disservice at the same time.

One could make a long list of words used lightly or in such a diluted or distorted sense that they convey very ambiguous and unhelpful messages. It is easy, for example, for a person to use words like *openness* and *truth* without much sensitivity to the many dimensions of meaning that are involved in them. Truth and openness currently possess an abrasive face for these people; they have become aggressive words, meant to dig into one's listeners as if salvation always comes through savage confrontation. Other words that are frequently used in a distorted and shallow way these days are *community, trust, beautiful, sexual* and *sharing.* Life demands more than that we merely pronounce these words, or any words for that matter. We speak words truly only when they flow from the mature level of our own experience.

The adult generation must preserve the meaning of these values in order to save man's sense of their profound significance. Man must stop speaking of them lightly or carelessly and look deeply into his own experience to understand them. In making the words that sum up our most important values his own again man will find himself and the fullness of life that can come only to those who are willing to enter into it very deeply.

DO YOU EVER HAVE THE FEELING . . . ?

NOT all the pacing about in confined quarters is done by lions in their cages. Men and women do it all the time when they are in the grip of a restlessness that just won't let them settle down. Symptom and response are curiously intermingled when the mood of restlessness is on us; we keep on the move in a variety of ways and these movements are both the sign of something out of joint inside us and the ineffective solution we try to apply to it.

When we are restless we find that it is difficult to concentrate on anything. We are always looking out the window, getting up to see if the mail has arrived, or perhaps rereading last night's newspaper, and we do all of these things with a studied but uncomprehending intensity. Sometimes we just drift around, feeling a little better as long as we are out of the chair in which we are supposed to be working, but not getting anywhere no matter how far we roam. Restlessness plagues the housewife, the bishop, and the executive indiscriminately. It makes them feel bad that they really don't feel better and it causes them to look for little jobs to do when there are big ones waiting for them.

There are many reasons for this easily recognized behavior. But when the spirit of restlessness is abroad in the land who can think hard or deep enough to analyze it? When somebody says to us, "What's the matter with you today anyway?" we are more than likely to answer, "I really don't know . . .," as we drift off to have another cigarette or another look out the window. It might be helpful the next time these all too human symptoms reappear in our own lives to take a little deeper look at ourselves and to try to understand what is really happening. Restlessness ordinarily points to some unfinished business in one's life, something with which one has yet to come to terms. As long as we delay it, or perhaps deny it altogether, there will be little progress elsewhere. Restlessness is one of the proofs that we cannot successfully dismiss or drown out what is really going on inside of ourselves.

Restlessness, for example, can be the result of some frustration, a frustration that we have pushed aside but that still has a grip on us. Restlessness can be a sign of foreboding, or it may result from some situation we do not want to face. It can point to a conflict, one that for some reason or other we really do not want to resolve. A man may have a disagreement with his wife which is unresolved as he heads off for work. It sputters and smolders and keeps him off balance all day. He may blame the weather or bad luck for his restlessness but he will not understand the real reason until he has worked through the difficulty with his wife. So too, a man may be in conflict because he has a difficult choice to make such as changing his job or buying a new house. These decisions can sometimes be so difficult that it is easier to keep delaying them. Restlessness will merely be the sign that he cannot successfully put off a conflict that must sooner or later be faced. Also, a man's restlessness may be his early reaction to something that is just over the horizon, a prophetic invitation to look in a new direction or accept a new challenge that has not quite formed clearly in his mind. Restlessness of this kind may, for example, be telling a man there is not enough meaning in his life, or that his relationships are not as deep as he thinks they are, or that there is more to his potential than he believes.

It is good to look in one or all of these directions before we give up or merely seek out some diversion that will distract us even further from the source of our restlessness. Restlessness, after all, may be pointing us in the direction of a richer life if we follow it down to its real roots inside ourselves. It is never cured by a holiday; there is nobody as unrefreshed as the vacationer whose restlessness makes the trip with him. In the long run, restlessness is the sign of a ragged edge in life or an undeveloped aspect of our personality. And a man need not be a genius nor spend a fortune on psychotherapy to begin to understand it. As Karen Horney once wrote, "Fortunately analysis is not the only way to resolve inner conflicts. Life itself remains a very effective therapist." The man who searches out the roots of his restlessness may discover that a fuller and more honest facing of life will cure it better than anything else. And he may also discover that his life can be far more wonderful than he ever suspected.

I DIDN'T KNOW YOU
WERE SO SENSITIVE

PEOPLE usually say that to us after they have made some remark that hurts us deeply. It is odd that they should be surprised to discover that, after they set out to hurt us, they really have caused us pain. Sometimes people play a dangerous game with their jests, skating a hazardous pattern across the thin crust of our self-esteem, hoping, with the excitement of a young boy on a winter pond, to get away with it. Others play the game from a distance, using greater subtlety and style; it is only when you turn your head to hear better that it falls off. Not everybody thinks he is as cutting as Don Rickles, but the phenomenon of persons relating through razor-edged put-downs is so universal that it bears a little closer inspection.

The put-down has become a style of relating in American culture, a substitute for richer and better things, a defensive mask to hide features shrivelled by loneliness, a cool way of staying loose and keeping people from getting too close. The very words "put-down" have an edge of malice in them; they are a sort of giveaway signal that this is not a game for good-natured friends as much as a stylized hostility that just looks as though it doesn't hurt. And, oddly enough, the fast remarks often drain off bad feelings that have little, if anything, to do with the person we put down. Our cleverness celebrates ourselves and some unresolved aspect of our own personality. The whole idea is to go one up by putting the other guy down. There is a strange self-serving dynamic at work here, a way of expressing our own discomfort while keeping others at a distance. People who relate this way develop a sixth sense for discovering the most vulnerable area of the other. It is not exactly a fair way to fight; it is a way of getting the other guy where it hurts him pretty badly. He is left bent over and holding himself, unable to fight back for a while.

Everybody knows persons who have learned "to keep others in their place" with their verbal anti-personnel weapons—those individuals who don't mean to hurt you but who do it just the same.

It is, in the long run, a bad business, leaving the attacker free of the others he has kept off so well, but also leaving him isolated. A sharp tongue is not much of a companion for a desperate old age. Maybe we ought to think of that the next time we are tempted to slaughter some innocent.

Then, too, there are things we can learn in the hand-to-hand combat that finally catches us just where we are weakest. There is something we can learn about ourselves from the sore points in our personality; a whole profile emerges from the tender reference points of our psyche. In other words, a little more courage to look at what we feel touchiest about may help us to know ourselves better. Often, the things we look away from are the very ones which betray us in life, those problem areas we could have approached and done something about if we had been a little less sensitive and a little more willing to learn.

Probably the most important thing we can learn from these situations is the power we ourselves have to hurt others, especially in close-range relationships with our family and with those we love. Putting people down is not much of a way to live; it is neither good psychology nor good philosophy. It certainly is not Christianity. We should resolve to become more conscious of the moments when we can really damage others and try to avoid these easy chances. We may hurt less, but everybody will be enjoying it more.

A MOMENT OF GRATITUDE

WE are all so distractible, or so lost in our own dreams and plans, that genuine gratitude is sometimes hard to generate and even harder to come by. Christ found that out the way most of us do, in human experience, when only one of the ten lepers came back to thank him for having been made clean. We are a funny race, we humans, always looking for something for ourselves, sometimes missing the best things when they are with us, and often too preoccupied to think of saying thanks for anything. If the Jesuit poet Gerard Manley Hopkins could "praise God for dappled things," perhaps we can find time to praise God for the simple things that are also the most profound things in life.

It is an old idea, of course, to remember that the stars and the sky belong to us all, as do fair days and first snowfalls. What we forget sometimes is that the real meaning of life lies in the quite common round of our experience, and that we need the time and occasion for putting this truth into perspective again. The only really poor people in this world are those who shield themselves from life and who can never give thanks for or celebrate life because they are not really a part of it.

Not many people have lives marked with high adventure or notable achievement; very few become famous or have monuments of gratitude raised in their names. They just go along, doing pretty much the same thing every day, dulled sometimes by the routine that is really the setting for the richest of all human experience. It is against the background of everyday life that people believe in and trust each other, that they love and give life to each other, that they try to do their best and leave things better for their children and grandchildren. Love, not fame or popularity, is what bridges the gaps of life and makes whole the lives of good people everywhere. To be present to each other in really sharing life is a far greater accomplishment than almost anything else a man can think of. Those who enter into the undramatic and everyday tasks of getting to know each other better, of raising a family, or serving others less selfishly—these are the same people who know that these experiences actually constitute the texture of life itself. They also understand happiness and how much there is really to be grateful for in life.

We need to see each other afresh and to realize how much of life lies in the living of it together. That is the strange thing about what is precious in life. We take each other for granted and we forget what gratefulness is for; we are so busy planning for the future or regretting the past that we often miss the quickly passing moments of sharing and struggle that are at the very heart of life. Love is not found in moments of high romance nearly as much as it is in times of simple sharing.

That is what Thornton Wilder, the author of *Our Town*, was getting at with his story of the day to day life in a little New England village. In one scene after her death, Emily, the young girl, learns that if she wishes she may return to life again. She is warned by the others in the cemetery that it will be a painful journey, but she selects a happy and ordinary day, her twelfth birthday. The stage-manager-narrator warns her. "You not only live it; but you watch yourself living it. . . . And as you watch it, you see the thing that they—down there—never know. You see the future. You know what's going to happen afterwards." Emily returns and speaks to the recreated past that cannot hear her, the past where people are going about their everyday tasks: "Oh, Mama, just look at me one minute as though you really saw me. Mama, fourteen years have gone by. I'm dead, You're a grandmother, Mama. . . . Wally's dead too. . . . We just felt terrible about it—don't you remember? But, just for a moment now we're all together, Mama, just for a moment we're happy. Let's look at one another. . . ."

Without too much self-consciousness we can sometimes look at one another gratefully if only for a moment. We can celebrate how much we share God's goodness in the love that makes us mean something to each other. We can recognize the fact that the life of the Spirit is not lived in any place but the regular round of trying to love each other a little more. We may not be able to keep this view of things in focus for long. To do so, however, even momentarily, will put the real values of life back into perspective for us. It is a simple vision but it is enough to move you deeply, enough to make you join with Emily who said, "Oh, earth, you're too wonderful for anybody to realize you. Do any human beings ever realize life while they live it?—every, every minute?"

RESCUE FANTASIES

THERE are people—some of them may be bearing down on you at this very moment—who want to save you from yourself by solving your problems for you. Now, that is all very well, you say, but where were they when I needed them, like last week when I was short of cash or last month when my in-laws came for a visit? We might as well be clear about these saviors right from the start. They do not respond to your need for help; they respond to their need to help you. It is quite possible—in fact, very likely—that your needs and their needs will not coincide. These proverbial helpers experience what psychiatrists and psychologists describe as "rescue fantasies." They live according to an imaginative picture of themselves charging off to snatch someone from an impending disaster. And the world is full of them.

The people who live by these heroic visions of themselves are not necessarily aware of their fantasy. It is so much a part of their make-up that they seldom reflect on it or look very deeply into themselves for its roots. Quite often they do a lot of good—and there is no sense in knocking good, even if it sometimes comes about in strange ways. The main problem with individuals motivated by rescue fantasies is that some of them cannot relate to people unless the people are in trouble; that is, they can give themselves to others only when the others are in some demonstrable need. And, instead of recognizing this need that they have to "rescue" others, they too often imagine that others are helpless and they rush to them with the bright light of "I'll save you" in their eyes.

There are times when we should give all the help and support to others that we can; but there are other times when it is best that we leave them alone. Ultimately, we must face up to and deal with our own problems by ourselves. Many times the overhelpful person spreading his rescue net beneath our lives is really denying us the chance to do something which, unless we do it for ourselves, will not effectively be accomplished. When we are in trouble, or even in deep sorrow, we need our friends around; they are the best friends, however, when they make themselves present but do not snatch our lives or our troubles out of our own hands. Our best friends, after all, are friends precisely because they know how to give themselves to us; that is what makes them different from the eager do-gooders who live by rescue fantasies.

What the latter do is take us over for themselves. They are the main characters in their wispy little visions of helping others. Their fantasies pull them like magnets from warm beds, quiet vacations, and pleasant home lives to rush to our side. But it is always the rescuer at our side who is really in the limelight, the person who really cannot live a normal and uninterrupted life and who contrives quite successfully not to. In fact, so good are they that you have a problem until they arrive at your side. It may, in the long run, be hard to tell whether the emergency attracts the rescue fancier or the rescue fancier attracts the emergency.

In any case, the man who lives by rushing off to solve other people's problems may sometimes do more harm than good. He has not yet learned that there are some things nobody can do much about, some emotions just too hot to touch, some wounds too tender to probe. At the same time, he may be leaving his own life in a relatively constant state of emergency, letting his own relationships deteriorate while he is busy trying to patch up those of others. The worst danger, then, is for the man who lives by these fantasies. They take him out of the real world, enable him to escape his more intimate responsibilities, and perpetuate the fiction that he is helping when he is actually only meddling. The next time you are tempted to think you are the only one who can save the world, or even your next door neighbor, think it over again. The mental health you save may be your own.

GALILEO WAS WRONG

INCREASING concern has been expressed about the "battered child syndrome" but precious little about the equally serious "battered man syndrome." While it is vital to respond to the terrible problem of children who are maltreated by their elders, it is also important to consider the elders who are mistreated by each other.

Not much good is said about man these days. Murphy's law that "anything that can go wrong will go wrong" prevails. Man is under multiple indictments and nobody even seems interested in making bail money for him. Add his own self-inflicted wounds and his penchant for pleading guilty to every charge, and one begins to understand his battered condition.

It is small wonder that men who really want to lead decent, loving, and law-abiding lives are discouraged. They have been accused of bulldozing down the past whose traditions they do not respect, polluting the present whose problems they do not understand, and of destroying the future whose promise they do not foresee. Modern man has shot down and stuffed the dove of peace, bartered away his sexual maturity for a mess of erotic pottage, and sacrificed his freedom to the gods of technology. Quite hung up, he has sold out, been taken in, and has little heart to break through. He is, it would seem, a quintessential disaster area.

Those who feel that the twentieth century is lived on the edge of a wide-open Pandora's box forget that the only good thing in that fabled container was hope. In their preoccupation with man the dupe, they have forgotten the power of hope, and the fact that man alone can experience and understand it. The pessimists have also lost touch with faith and love and what man is like at his best.

It is not surprising that modern men beat against the bars of the rational grid which technology has clamped over their living space. They have, for example, revived astrology, searching the numb and frozen stars for direction. But man is not made intelligible by the stars. Quite the reverse is true. The stars are made intelligible by the mind of man. They are charted on the map that issues from human intelligence.

To the confounding of Galileo, man, not the sun, is the center of the universe. Man dominates creation, teasing out its secrets and working its energy to his own purpose. Too many critics have forgotten man's place in the scheme of things and so they have also forgotten his promise and his possibilities.

It is said that at one point in their history the Greeks turned to the stars for direction because it was easier to surrender to them than to accept responsibility for themselves. Man is at that point again; he can be overwhelmed by the burden of his errors, or he can take charge of himself and his destiny once more. The Christian cannot choose fatalism and despair. The greatest reality for him is that man lives at the center of a redeemed universe and the Spirit, not the stars, is the source of his strength.

Men, scarred by violence and war, confused by the pain of so much of their own personal experience, are trying to remember what they are really like. They seem as innocent children who have learned too much, longing for the strengths they seemed to have in simpler times. Christians cannot stand around weeping for themselves and their children as they look for the Lord in the skies. They are responsible for man and for sharing with him the eternal freshness of the Gospels. The Gospels, it must be remembered, are good news.

In the twenty-fifth chapter of St. Matthew, the saved, in the setting of the last judgment, ask the Lord, "When did we see you hungry and feed you; or thirsty and give you drink? When did we see you a stranger and make you welcome; naked and clothe you; sick or in prison and go to see you?" There is a contemporary answer to that. It is the now generation that hungers and thirsts for an understanding of themselves and their place in the panorama of creation. They are strangers in the double-grip of loneliness and alienation; naked, when exposed to a punishing and contrary world; sick, when they have lost touch with their wholeness; in prison when they are bound by superstition and inhuman philosophies of life. Battered man needs the good news more than he ever has before.

In a world where things are made to wear out, men are searching for the things that last. Good men, lost for the moment in their tortured journeyings, not only need but want an understanding of faith, hope, and love. These are the interpersonal virtues, the ones that touch the most valued and basic experiences of their lives. The experience of faith, hope and love gives man life, the measure of his meaning, and the fulfillment of his longings for spiritual and personal fulfillment. Although their source is the Spirit, these things that last are found only in man's relationship with his fellow man. Life is lived with each other or it isn't lived at all.

Only battered man lives the life of the Spirit. With all his well-documented faults and missteps, he alone, of all created things, is the instrument through which the Spirit transforms the face of the earth. Religion, then, is centered in man's struggle to believe even when he can be betrayed, to hope even when he can be disappointed, and to love even when he can be hurt in the effort. The Gospels say that this is possible for man and that it is available for him if he opens himself to the Spirit.

Man reaches into space but he can also reach into himself. He is not likely to succeed in either endeavor if he looks only at the bad news, blames others for his problems, or surrenders to the sway of the stars. The Gospels, and the Church that rises from them, are for pilgrim man. Our fulfillment comes from our commitment to the good news, not to keep it to ourselves, but to share it with battered but lovable man.

A FEW KIND WORDS FOR LOSERS

THERE is nothing Americans love more, the old saying goes, than a winner. But where, given the relatively small supply of first places available, does that leave most of us who may not have the chance, the skill, or even the dumb luck to ever win anything except a bamboo backscratcher at a church bazaar? Who, after all, wins the Lincoln Continental, the mink stole and the trip for two to Europe and beyond? That's right; somebody who bought only one raffle ticket, the lady who has a mink stole already, and the same couple who won the kitchenful of appliances last year. But you? Never. Along with a large, shuffling and anonymous army, you have somehow missed first place money in all your years of going to school, playing amateur sports, or buying chance books.

According to legions of Americans who when they don't think they look like John Wayne imagine that they at least sound like the late Vince Lombardi, winning is everything. While we like good losers we don't make much room for them in our affections or our sports pages. But there is more losing in life than there is winning, and the person who does not realize this just invites bitterness and frustration into his life. Furthermore, it may be that we have gone much too far in justifying almost any kind of behavior as long as it leads to winning. Lying, cheating, knifing others in the back in the climb to the top—we have had enough of these to last us the rest of the century. We are so psyched up for winning that even the tragic war we are involved in puzzles and frustrates us because of our failure to achieve the decisive triumph we have always savored—a failure that may possibly be good for the national soul.

On the other hand, we have been so disillusioned about the impossibility of winning, not only at war, but even at life and love, that we have come to celebrate the loser, the non-hero, the dropout who steps out of life because he prefers to think that it does not really mean anything anyway. These people flood our movies, our books and, according to some accounts, our choicest national parks. The hard winner and the born loser—they seem so different, and yet a closer inspection reveals that they are at least second cousins if not exactly blood brothers.

The one is so wrapped up in winning that he avoids competition by trying to fix the outcome in some way or other; fair fights, after all, are not for him and the end justifies the means, no matter how questionable the means may be. He does not really face life on its terms. He writes his own scenario, cuing the scenes so that the action works out the way he wants it. In his heart, you see, he is not a competitor. He is just deathly afraid of losing. And when, by whatever means, he wins, he is deathly afraid that he will lose what he has acquired. The drop-out is terrified of losing too, terrified of showing that he cares, and so he chooses a course that protects him from failure through competiton by embracing failure as a vocation. Neither of these characters is very normal or productive.

But there are other kinds of losers too, the individuals who believe in something and do their best to achieve it, even against great odds. They cannot always win either but they sleep peacefully because they live honorably. It is just that we have little time for these people, and too often not enough recognition of their integrity and their character. People who compete fairly on the basis of their convictions and from their inner courage may not enjoy the experience of losing but it does not terrify or destroy them either. They live by a mature set of values and they give us a model for the way a Christian must live.

Those who live by faith commit themselves to a course where they are always in danger of losing everything. This is the down-to-earth experience of persons who try to live by the Spirit and who find that this frequently leads them along a narrow path where they are vulnerable to the massed forces of defeat and discouragement. Christians who are promised that their faith will overcome the world do not imagine that this will be accomplished through military conquest or some modern-day miracles that will astonish and humble the rest of mankind. They know, through the sort of wisdom wrought by the spirit, that the world is overcome only by those who are prepared to lose themselves in loving and serving it. The Christian possesses the very things that all men yearn for, the values that cannot be acquired by either the ruthless or the passive, the things you really do not lose even when you give them away. And these are the qualities of life that so many people have indeed lost and cannot seem to find again. The Christian gives of his belief to the man who has lost faith in himself, in life, in any kind of God; the Christian gives of his hope to the man who has given up on finding any good anywhere at all; the Christian gives of his love to those who think they have lost it forever. A deep and central element of the Christian message is the mystery of being ready to die in order that others may discover life, being ready to risk everything, not foolishly or impulsively, but purposefully for the sake of other men. The man who insists on winning and the man who insists on losing can never understand that at all. But this mystery, this incredible reality of the everyday Christian life, is the great sign of faith that overcomes and reconciles the world at last.

MURDEROUS TRUTH

THE fast-closing sixties have proved to be years in which we have relearned the original meaning of the word encounter. When first used, it signified "to meet an enemy." The encounters of the recent past, both on a social and an individual level, have put a premium on an assaulting kind of authenticity, on telling it like it is by attacking you as you are. The passion for truth à la "Virginia Woolf" is acted out on many of life's stages: in the protests in the streets and on the campuses, in certain species of group dynamics, and in living rooms and bedrooms all across the land.

It is obviously a good thing to tell the truth and to establish relationships on the basis of what is real rather than what is false about ourselves. But the truth, as St. Augustine long ago noted, can be "murderous" when it is used as a weapon. We have certainly reached the age of overkill in confronting each other. Indeed, it is perhaps time to wonder whether all the supposed forthrightness, all the demanded authenticity, have really contributed to better human relationships or not. A man can, after all, use the truth, not to reach another, but to separate himself from another; it can make us free but it can also enslave us to our own inner hostility when it is used merely to overwhelm other people. Honesty is the best policy, but honesty can get lost in our anger, and turn out to be a poor policy indeed. Honesty in dealing with each other demands a seasoning of human understanding and a feeling for each other's weakness. We don't have to destroy each other to share the truth with each other.

Indeed, the very word sensitivity has, because of the popularity of some styles of encounter groups, almost become a synonym for the exchange of harsh but presumably liberating truth. True sensitivity, however, means being able to see into the world of the other, being able to forgive and take into account the other person's weakness, offering compassion rather than confrontation. Compassion is woefully missing in many contemporary champions of authentic dialogue. Somewhat unforgiving of the human condition, they look on sympathy as a weakness and mercy as a mistake. Psyches stripped raw, personal wounds kept open, weaknesses magnified—these are the elements of the modern day murderous truth. Why are they this way? Well, it is still true that the best defense is a good offense. Attacking others excuses them from the far more difficult business of understanding those they confront; it oversimplifies life and masks its complexity; it gives them power and control over others.

But not everybody can handle the whole truth about themselves all at once. Indeed, experience in psychotherapy shows that confronting another is a very delicate business that requires great skill and sensitivity to whether the other is strong enough to handle it. Sometimes a premature confrontation closes off rather than opens up another person. And to confront others too savagely may lead them to leave therapy rather than make progress in it. The skilled therapist also knows that he must be prepared to stick with the person after he has shared some truth with him in order to help him understand and assimilate it successfully. All this is very different from the "hit and run, take it or leave it, now it's your problem" approach of the purveyors of murderous truth.

The truly sensitive person is no less committed to the truth but he understands that the truth must be shared in a human manner. Sometimes the other person is just too weak at the moment to stand another body blow. A real concern for fallible human beings makes us put them, at times, ahead of the naked truth. What is the truth to a person who cannot yet hear it, or who will not yet lower his defenses to look at it? What does the savage expression of truth, the quick slit of the jugular, do to a person who is just too played out emotionally to handle it? There may be, along with a time for war and a time for peace, a time for letting people hold on to their illusions a little longer. Maybe these illusions are the only things that are holding them together; maybe these are the only things that they have left. Christ spoke of not extinguishing the candle that was sputtering low and not breaking the already bruised reed.

I think often of the story a young man told me once about his father, a wealthy black businessman. It seems that his father found one of his employees cheating and had to let him go. A few days later the discharged employee's wife came to see the boy's father with fire in her eyes. Her husband had not been dishonest, she claimed, it was the boy's father who was at fault. She went on and on, berating the man while she staunchly defended her husband. All through it the boy's father listened patiently and tried to indicate how much he understood her concern and her loyalty to her husband. After she had left, the boy asked his father why he had not told her the truth, why he had not produced all the proof of the many thefts of which the man had been guilty. The father replied, "Son, that man is no good and is going to break her heart more. But right now he's the only thing she's got to believe in. What would it do to her to take that away?"

Maybe not many of us can be that understanding or that Christian, especially when we have the proof of how right we are about something. But we can all learn something about compassion and a feeling for each other's weakness from this man's example. It is probably accurate to realize that the truth can always hurt, but there is something of the Gospel in realizing that it is not meant to be a deadly weapon.

WHOEVER SAID WE WERE
SUPPOSED TO BE EFFICIENT?

THE hills are alive not with music but with experts trying to make the world run better. Look in the Yellow Pages under *management consultants* and you will find, in the big cities at least, a yard or two of them. Americans have always been big on efficiency, time-motion studies, better mouse traps, higher compression ratios in their engines, zip codes and area codes—these have been a part of our national bag for a long time now. Search the bookshelves and every publishing season will find another set of books on new and improved methods of management. Go to conventions and you will find that what is proclaimed as new is also proclaimed as efficient. But, stop right there a moment and think about whether we are, any of us, really very efficient after all.

As a matter of disquieting fact the world seldom runs efficiently. That is why there is always a market for those who would try, in each succeeding generation, to teach the world the lessons of efficiency all over again. The world did not come into existence very efficiently. Despite the reputation of the architect, there was no sharp, clean, or economical use of the materials at hand. It would never be as beautiful as it is if the world had been designed with an eye on the clock or the balance sheet. The world would probably look like an endless version of Park Avenue, whose glass-sheathed buildings are indistinguishable, efficient and ice-cold. Human beings do not grow in an efficient manner; they come in all shapes and sizes, at varying rates and with varying gifts, the despair of any efficiency-minded designer. Their growth comes in unexpected ways and at unpredictable moments. Persons, however, grow in the only way that is good for man, the human way.

Efficiency experts often forget that what seems efficient for man on the drawingboard is not necessarily efficient in real life. It is very efficient, for example, to code everything in a hospital to a number given to the patient upon his arrival. But it can be very dispiriting to the patient, already stripped of his clothes and personal effects, to be treated that way. It is very efficient, or so it seems, to design modern kitchens bristling with gadgets. Take the oven, for example. It looks like the cockpit of a 747 these days, with remote control devices, unnumbered thermometers, and at least another handful of dials and clocks, all designed to fit neatly into the context of high speed, efficient America. Recent studies have shown, however, that the average American housewife does not use most of this equipment, that she prefers to blunder along, something like her grandmother, poking straws in things, sampling sauces with the tip of her finger, and cooking in the only way that she finds comfortable. That is the efficient way for her because it is the only way for her. It seems that these kitchens are mostly designed by male engineers who love efficient machines but who never had to cook a meal in their lives. There is a glorious triumph for humanity in the kitchens of America, where so many sophisticated dials, like blinded electronic eyes, stare dully into space.

The world, when you take a close look at it, just does not run efficiently at all. Politicians have understood this for centuries and they have kept governments going, not by being efficient, but by dealing with men as they are. The men who really understand the basic inefficiency of mankind are called diplomats or statesmen. Politics, defined as the art of the possible, is that precisely because it is built on an understanding of the way things are actually accomplished in the human condition. Anybody, be he executive, politician or pope, who thinks that he will be able to eliminate all reduplication and get everything on a smooth and businesslike basis for any great period of time, is bound to be frustrated if he is not ready to settle for less. That is why the battle goes on, the experts at efficiency blazing new and direct trails to the goals they can define so clearly, while the jungle gradually closes in again just a few steps behind them.

This is not cynicism; it is merely a reflection on the fact, were we to admit it, that most of us do things humanly, that is to say inefficiently, when we do them at all. It is hard to teach old dogs new tricks. That is why the rising generation can always accuse the retiring generation of some measure of inefficiency and feel wonderfully self-righteous about it. It is a safe accusation to make against any generation because it is true of all of them. Even the Third Reich, fabled as such a highly organized political and war machine, turns out, in the memoirs of Albert Speer, Hitler's Minister of Armaments, to have been as badly managed a government as the world is likely to see. Speer was efficient and became famous for keeping production levels rising throughout the war despite the allied bombings. One of the reasons he was able to do this was the vast inefficiency of the government in keeping records of war material. Speer could always find more material because the information was so poorly kept—throughout the Reich inaccurate estimates of supplies were the rule rather than the exception. But all that his efficiency accomplished was to keep the war going long after it would otherwise have far more humanly ended. Haven't you ever wondered at how the economy keeps going, given the state of the average man's bookkeeping? Perhaps Robert Frost was right when he wrote that "Nobody was ever meant to remember or invent what he did with every cent."

Perhaps the churches, now eagerly turning to management consultants, financial disclosures, and other moves toward efficiency, should ponder the realities of the inefficiency of the human condition. You may remember the research done about a dozen years ago to compare the world's organizations for efficiency. The Roman Catholic Church was rated second, right behind one of the great U.S. oil companies. That either tells you a lot about all the other companies of the world, or it tells you something about research. In any case, the churches might examine themselves on whether they really want to make efficiency the sign of their renewal and their relevance. The church, after all, is a place in which people are meant to feel at home, a place where, with the spiritual help the church can give, they can grow to their full manhood in Christ Jesus.

The places in which we know that men can grow are not really the most efficient of situations. Men grow in the family, that beleaguered institution that has never been accused of efficiency. Indeed, parents who try to make their households into efficient operations replete with timetables and schedules often raise rather mechanical children who walk woodenly and unimaginatively through life. Where else does growth take place? Men and women grow when they fall in love and this process also has never had high marks for efficiency. It preoccupies and drains a man of his energy, making him moon around during hours when he should be working; and yet it is still the best experience he knows, the experience that opens up the magic of the world to him. When you come to think of it, Christ did not seem to worry much about efficiency either. He would have had himself born in the electronic age if he thought that the most efficient means of conveying the Good News was more important than the substance of that message. And he probably would not have gone around breaking and using up whole jars of oil or letting the apostle that would betray him carry the purse.

Christ lived an intensely human life and he invites us to do the same thing. That is the whole meaning of Incarnation, and the current soul-searching of the churches is leading them all to examine the implications of this. It does not seem wise to pursue renewal solely in terms of making the operations of the churches more efficient. That is a praiseworthy goal but it can never be the most important one for preachers of the Gospel who are trying to help people find and share themselves as a community led by the Spirit. Maybe the Spirit can only touch us and change us when we drop the armor of efficiency and are able to let ourselves out with all the rough edges of life showing. And maybe we harden our hearts to the Spirit when we begin to worship the cool uncaring gods of hardnosed efficiency. The churches' current romance with management consultants sounds like the right thing until you think a little more about it. The churches can stand a little more human inefficiency if they commit themselves wholeheartedly to the task they cannot accomplish efficiently anyway, that of making a family of mankind under the breath of the Spirit.

THERE IS NOTHING
PERSONAL IN THIS . . .

NOT much, there isn't. Few phrases in the language mean nearly the opposite of what they seem to say on the surface as much as this one. It is hardly ever used except in those situations in which there is something highly personal involved; it is a banner with a strange device indeed, a red flag snapping from the lance of the conversationalist who uses it, a small craft warning, if you will, telling you that a storm is about to break on your head. People use these words only when the current of personal feeling within them is running so strong that they have to defend themselves against it lest it overwhelm them. They must reassure themselves of their objectivity, remind themselves of their fairness, maintain control, and hope that you do too, when they are really pretty damned mad at you in a very personal way.

Just think of the last time you used the phrase yourself. If there was nothing personal in it, then why did you have to reassure yourself about it? If it was all quite objective, why preface your remarks by such a statement? Things that are not personal do not sound personal when they come out; things that are personal, sound that way no matter how much we may deny it.

There are a few lessons to be learned from this style of remark (it has other faces too, such as, "Don't get me wrong. I really like you." Or, "We've always seen eye to eye so I know you won't misunderstand if I tell you . . ."). First of all, if you find yourself saying it, then it might be good to re-examine yourself and your feelings before you go any farther. With strong personal feelings heated up, you may say more than you wish and you will probably aggravate rather than clear up the condition you propose to discuss with the other person. If you are the person to whom the remark is made, then try to avoid getting as defensive as the words are likely to make you. If you get upset, then the other person has got you just where he wants you. If you're going to be as wise as the biblical serpent, if not exactly as guileless as the dove, check the personal feelings that will immediately rise up in you. Listen more than you speak and realize that it is a highly personal communication and that, despite the disclaimer, the subject cannot really be discussed objectively at the moment. If you try to avoid the tactics that will only heighten the emotional strain between you and the other, you may eventually be able to get to some mutual high ground on which you can discuss the situation. Wading right in while there are live wires down all around you has never been a very promising policy.

It would be hard to estimate the number of disastrous and unproductive confrontations that could be avoided if people read accurately the emotional semaphore they wigwag to themselves and others in such subtle ways. The language of emotion is the one that carries the meaning we have as persons in our relationships with others, and we give off messages about it even when our words are saying something else. So watch for the signals and do not pretend to be objective, one way or the other, when you are really being intensively subjective. Things will go much better in the long run for all concerned. And remember, there's nothing personal in all this.

PRIDE

PEOPLE don't talk about pride much anymore, or even about the capital sins, among which pride was *primus inter pares*. The probable reason why pride has fallen into disfavor is that it was overused as an explanation for our perversity. When I was in the seminary it was the all-purpose vice, the sure diagnosis for every spiritual illness. Like the common cold, there was a lot of it going around in the old days of ten-day retreats and silent prayer.

In fact, pride was the most pursued of vices, just as humility was the most pursued of virtues. There was at times a kind of competition among the devout to dig out pride from the nooks and crannies of the soul where it readily took root. And humility, to think of oneself as nothing, was the DDT to kill it off. Now, just as we are wary of the overuse of DDT, many Christians are afraid they overdid humility in the battle against pride. The self was always under siege and was valued so little that many discovered that they had seriously undermined their own self-confidence. Small wonder that there is so much talk about fulfillment and the development of the individual personality these days; it is a reaction to the highly negative attacks launched against the self to overcome pride.

Pride still lives, of course, although it isn't an intellectual vice, even though it has often been described that way. For that matter, it isn't even all bad. Pride is more a feeling about ourselves than a way of thinking about ourselves. As such, it is the product of the way we use our personalities in the labor and love of life. When we use ourselves well, we have a good feeling about it, a kind of pride that flows from fitting together in relationship to ourselves and to others. That is a healthy feeling, the feedback that is akin to the pride of workmanship, the emotional evidence of a person who is loving himself rightly. A man who is trying his best will experience a wholesome pride that is quiet and filled with peace.

Pride that is distorted and destructive arises from false premises about the self. It is a feeling about ourselves that is so inflated and pervasive that it edges everybody else out of our lives. The victim of this type of pride does not know himself, and cannot love himself in an integrated way; he can only defend himself against his own distortions. It is very difficult for this kind of proud man to love. He would rather go down in the loneliness of his self-infatuation than make room for his real self or for others in his life. Men have been known to be too proud to fight and too proud to beg; the most melancholy man of all is the one who is too proud to love.

Pride, in this extreme form, chokes off life because it closes a man off from others. The sinfully proud man plunders the personalities around him, feeding himself but failing to nourish others. His pride is a defense against seeing the truth of what he does to himself and to others. This kind of pride runs deeper than the vanity that makes a man concerned about the way he looks on the outside. That kind of vanity is common and forgivable; the pride that shuts out others is not so common and is always deadly.

Indeed, the problem is not the deadly proud man who nuzzles comfortably into the lining of his own ego. It is, rather, that we have so few people with a healthy sense of pride in themselves and that we have so many whose feelings are characterized not by overconfidence but by underconfidence in themselves. This lack of confidence in people may be partially the fruit of all those years of beating the supposed badness of pride out of them. It may be complicated by the pervading sense that so many things in life seem to have gotten beyond our control. In any case, this lack of trust in the self, this nonpride of self-alienation, is practically an epidemic in the land today.

This underconfident person never gets to know *himself* very well either and so he never really tests his strength in the struggle of life. There is some evidence to suggest that those who never really tap their own resources hold back from life out of fear of failure. To avoid the painful consequences of a public setback, they do not involve themselves at all. They shift uneasily on the edge of life, waiting for the right moment when no one will laugh at them and no one will criticize them. They use a perfectionistic defense, always putting off doing this or that until they are sure they have it planned so that they will be immune from criticism. But they never get it perfect enough and so they never get very much done either. Waiting for the moment of no risk at all, these people are always on the sidelines but never really in the game.

The really capital sin, if such a term can be used, is this passive and fearful nonparticipation more than it is any overbearing kind of pride. The mock humility of some of these people covers up their desire to neutralize the conditions of life so that they are never in danger. But that is to turn away from life altogether. St. Thomas once asked the question of whether it would be better to ask a proud or a fearful person to do something. He said that he would choose the proud man because then at least something would be done. The fearful man, on the other hand, is overcome by caution and he avoids mistakes by avoiding action altogether.

Fear that has not been faced lies beneath the problems of the persons who have not learned to trust themselves or take a healthy pride in making their best effort, even if it is imperfect. These people have a lot of trouble loving others, too. That is because love subjects us to the biggest risks of all, the danger of being bruised and disappointed by the ones we love. Right now the world and the Church need people who are ready to run some risks, even the risk of being a little proud, for the sake of loving more. A capital sin is committed when the good news of the Gospel goes unpreached because people have been too fearful of life to enter into it. Pride won't be the cause of that as much as the faintheartedness of those who think they are humble when they are really only scared.

THE LAST TIME I SAW HARRIS . . .

. . . HE looked a lot different than the first time I saw him. Then he was the kind of person you hardly notice, the type you could barely locate in time and space although you had met him the day before, a slender young man with a complexion like fieldstone, a slightly bumbling fellow who seemed always to be backing away and apologizing for something. He was, in fact, a graduate student nearing the end of his doctoral research at a large university. He was 25 years old and as intellectually sharp as he was socially awkward. It was not so surprising that he was quiet and passive; he had never moved out of his parents' home, never even been away from them overnight. They made all the decisions for him, even the simplest, telling him what time to go to church and generally supervising his life in a seemingly benevolent but very strict way. There was an unbelievable note of pathos in the fact that his father still selected and tied his tie for him every morning. He was a sad person, an undeveloped and naive young man you would be afraid to let go downtown by himself, practically a non-person who was at the same time vulnerable to and unprepared for the inevitable rudeness of life.

But Harris began to get anxious about his future and the fact that he would soon have to get a job, anxious enough to consult the university psychiatrist for some advice. In the therapist's office this forlorn young man began pecking at the shell in which he had been transported through life so far. Because the psychiatrist was both compassionate and skillful Harris began to identify for himself exactly what had happened and not happened to him during his first quarter century of life. He sensed his own capitulation to parental domination, a major factor with which he had never dealt, and he began to feel the frustration and pain that had built up inside himself during all those years. It was hard for him to speak about his mother and father; it is hard for everybody. He loved them and did not want to hurt them but he knew also that he had to begin, howsoever clumsily, to make a life of his own. He had, almost literally, to be born again, but this time he had to be his own obstetrician.

It would be nice to say that Harris moved quickly and surely through psychotherapy, making new friends and influencing people as he set his course toward the open sea of a happy-ever-after life. This was not so. It is hardly ever so for anybody who opens himself to growth. For Harris there were pains and disappointments far deeper than any he had known during the sheltered years of his life. What was different was the new way he had of responding to these difficulties, the more constructive reactions that made these events into sources of continued development.

For example, Harris, in opening up to himself in therapy, found that it was possible to open up to other people a little more as well. Other people began to come into his field of vision not merely as objects in space but as persons in their own right, persons who were suddenly filled with magic and wonder for him. He pushed himself to talk to another graduate student, a bright young lady who responded with a certain amount of sympathy to his struggling presentation of himself. For the first time in his life Harris made a date with a girl; it was really the first time he found himself reacting warmly to a woman; and in short order it was the first time he fell in love. Love showered on him like the April rain and, with stars in his eyes and a spirit of adventure that had never entered his soul before, he put himself out to find just the right flowers, the kind of candy, even the brand of dinner wine she preferred. He even bought a new tie and mastered the art of knotting it for himself.

Everybody warned him not to get too involved, everybody, that is, who began to notice the transformations occurring in this shy young man. He even realized that he was investing too much himself, but it was so different from anything he had ever known, and it made him feel so good, that he plunged ahead heedlessly. It was at this point that yet another graduate student, a semi-friend of Harris', noticed the young lady too. With some malice aforethought he went after her himself. And that was the end of Harris' beginning romance, a fiery crash on his first flight, and shot down by someone on his own side. Everybody who knew him shuddered and covered his eyes, feeling that the sight of Harris the failed lover would be too painful to look at.

But Harris was beginning to discover inner strengths that he never knew existed before, and while he was nearly crushed by the abrupt end of his first romance he was also determined not to let his passivity get the better of him again. He decided to keep in touch with the girl rather than to hide away from the situation that had caused him so much heartbreak. And he was going to attend a convention of his specialty and get himself a job. This latter resolve was as big a step as he had ever taken because it meant that he would have to be away from home and on his own for three days. It was not easy, but Harris, supported by his therapist, launched into the economic deep and started to swim like a man intent on saving himself. He landed a job at a college a thousand miles away and shortly had to make another trip to see it for himself and to be interviewed. Harris was alive again, struggling with life rather than succumbing to the security his protective parents seemed to offer.

When Harris got back, job in hand, he called the girl he had briefly dated and asked her if she would like to go to the movies that night. No, she said, she was too tired. Well, then, how about the next night? She was all booked up, she said. A few days later Harris met her on the campus and she told him she was free that evening if he still wanted to take her to the show. But something had changed in Harris, and he didn't need her to survive. No, he told her, I'm booked up myself. Maybe some other time.

Harris had come a long way in the months in which he had combined the experience of psychotherapy with his first frontal assault on life. A long way indeed, because a little boy had turned into a growing young man. He is far from fully grown even now. His parents are planning to move along with him to his new job and he has not had any new girl friends lately. But Harris, the last time I saw him, was doing battle with life and finding much more of himself in the process. He is a model, in a way, for everybody who has ever had a hurt or who has had to start all over at some point in life. Harris is growing and there are other problems lying in wait for him. But nobody can take his growth away from him.

HOW TO LEARN ABOUT
YOURSELF WITHOUT TRYING

GETTING to know yourself has never been much fun. Taking a good look at one's self has usually been classified with such joyous tasks as taking a cold shower or sipping bad medicine—one makes a lot of faces to get through these supposedly salutary experiences. Self-knowledge is usually served up as an enterprise so serious and emotionally involving that a person can get discouraged just thinking about it. There must be some middle way between the mechanical and highly intellectual examination of conscience and the bosom-bearing confrontation of an encounter group. Why can't self-knowledge be slow and easy, something like losing weight without exercising or growing wise without studying?

For those men who are already harried enough by late twentieth century existence, we present some suggestions for learning about yourself without really trying. You know how it is sometimes; you get a sudden glimpse of yourself in a store window as you are passing by and, from that shimmering reflection, you learn more about yourself than you have learned in years. Well, the world is full of psychological windowpanes that reflect our true selves; we just have to learn where and when to glance.

For example, somewhat in the manner of a good cameraman, the next time you are stopped at a red light, focus on yourself. In those few moments when you feel that no one is watching you, you are usually as freely yourself as you are likely to be all day long. You use no psychological defenses because there is no one to guard against and no one to impress. You may find yourself scratching your nose but that bit of realism may tell you more than you anticipated. If you don't like that picture, cut to yourself seated at a banquet table listening to a talk, or to your church pew as you listen to a sermon. We become ourselves as we become more distracted, and if you look behind that set face on the silver screen of your imagination, your projected fantasies will tell you a lot about yourself. Failing that, try to get some perspective on yourself the next time you are standing at a cocktail party not really listening to the person who is talking to you. Look closely and see if you can sense where you would really rather be as you are nodding "Yes, yes" with that blank smile on your face. That will also tell you something you didn't know before.

If none of these suggestions work, try to finish the following sentence in ten words: "I would really like to. . . ." Whatever just came to your mind is informative about your genuine personality. We are always letting ourselves out. It is just that we have not learned when we can best see and understand ourselves. So, carefully look at and listen to yourself in those quiet moments when you think you are standing in the wings rather than on the stage of life. You can learn something valuable; nobody else will know it and it hardly hurts at all. Void where prohibited by law.

EVERYTHING HURTS SOMEBODY SOMETIME

OF all the sighs of life, none is more heartfelt than the one we breathe when we are emotionally hurt by others. Being emotionally offended in a profoundly painful experience, so human and yet so common that everybody knows the feeling firsthand. Most of us put emphasis on the times we have suffered hurt rather than on the times we have been the cause of it. We are, while the breath of life is in us, always on the edge of being involved in it. Hurting and being hurt are combustible elements of the human condition; there is always some danger but, were they absent, we would not be human at all.

Some people trade their humanity for insulation from the chance possibility of being hurt. They close their hatches and plunge far beneath life's surface, chasing the shadows of the depths to avoid anyone who seems to them a hunter. They can never get deeply enough away, however, as their own loneliness, like a recurrent fever, reminds them.

There is something infinitely poignant about their defensive maneuvers, just as there is something wrenchingly sad about the testimony they give of themselves. Nobody's cash is as cold as that of the well-known billionaire who, in response to a question about his many marriages, said, "I've always tried to avoid being hurt. It doesn't do you any good, letting a woman get to you that badly. I've been pretty successful at avoiding being hurt, I think."

You really give up too much of life, no matter how much you gather in gold, when you try to eliminate hurt from your experience. It is only when we can be touched deeply by another that we are open enough to life to understand its meaning at all. That is not an easy saying, despite all that is written these days about the risk of real loving. For, common as hurt is, it is a hard thing to handle. It cannot be ignored and it cannot be laughed off. Sometimes, because of circumstances, there is nothing we can do but feel the pain of it, the throbbing throughout our person that won't go away no matter how we try to distract ourselves.

This is what happens when we are hurt by the person we love most, the one to whom we usually come when emotionally wounded and misunderstood by others. There is no hurt like this one. This misunderstanding, no matter how momentary, cuts so deeply that we cannot even speak without making it hurt more. It is the hurt that can make us back away from each other, from those we trust and hold most dear, as if some cruel fate has suddenly made us into strangers again. Time brings things back into focus, but there are no moments lonelier than those when hurt comes from the ones we love.

The reason for this is clear enough, whether it happens between husband and wife, old friends, or young lovers looking forward to a life together. Love and trust, when they are real, make us lower our guard and open our real selves to others; we are most vulnerable to our beloved, most defenseless with those we really love most. That is why the pain is so intense. We do not have any defenses up, nothing to shield us from the blow, no matter how accidentally it is delivered. We can only feel the full force of it, and hear the very breath being knocked out of us at the same time. We can, in moments of such hurt, feel misunderstanding like a hot blade cutting through our innards.

At times like these, times we try to avoid as much as possible, we might think of the fact that this is the way the persons we love feel when for one reason or another, we hurt them. When we know the measure of such hurt, we may become more careful not to inflict this kind of suffering on others. Much thoughtlessness goes into some of the deepest hurts of life. Nobody really means to hurt the other, especially when the other is near and dear, and yet we go right on doing it all the time. There are all kinds of cuts, kind and unkind, that we give others without really noticing it. We have to work hard for the maturity that makes us aware of what a deadly weapon our own thoughtlessness can be.

There has been a lot of loose talk in the United States lately about how we all share some corporate guilt for this or that event, from assassinations to the generation gap. It is really much easier to make that kind of global accusation against ourselves than to face the real injuries we do quite personally to one another. The latter is hard because we know the sting of hurt and it is not pleasant to think that we can hand the same thing on to others.

Some of us even like to feel sorry for ourselves and to nurse our hurts as long as we can. That is why, I think, Christ made so much of wholehearted forgiveness.

There would be no healing for us at all unless we could grant each other real forgiveness. That is not easy because, once we are hurt, we are likely to keep our guard up for a while afterwards. But real forgiveness, the Christian element that restores wholeness to people, is given only if we are willing to drop our guard once more. Forgiveness demands that we make ourselves open to getting hurt all over again. That asks a great deal from each of us, much more than a quick *mea culpa* or an embarrassed wish that we would forget that this or that has happened. Forgiveness comes from people who have hurt each other but are willing, out of the love that gives them that awful power still, to run the risk that it may happen again. That is the only remedy there is for the hurts we give to one another.

The scar tissue on lovers' hearts is the sign of the two-edged power of love itself. It is only because love makes us so open and trusting that it also makes us targets for each others' occasional insensitivity. It is through the power of that same love, a gift of the Spirit, that we can bring our faith in each other to even greater fullness. And that is the faith that makes men whole. Love is what holds our lives together and strengthens us for the hazards of the life in which everybody hurts somebody sometime. We are all responsible for seeing that the human family, full of hurts and aches, experiences more of the loving forgiveness that is written about in the Gospels.

DOLDRUMS AND DEPRESSIONS

THE strangest things settle in on us in the summertime. Just when we ought to be carefree, recovering from the long winter behind us and storing up energy for the season just ahead, we sometimes find ourselves suddenly and inexplicably down in the dumps. Everything can be going fine when, all of a sudden, we turn our head and the world looks different. The wind slackens and our sails collapse; what we had anticipated we now have little feeling for at all. The Penn Central has nothing on us for a quick and unexpected bankruptcy of the spirit. It is a seasonal illness, the kind of depression that grabs us when we ease up a little, the specter that rises up to let us down right in the middle of our holidays.

There is nothing unusual about this kind of experience; it is the sort of thing we shrug off in the busier months when the clock leaves few hours for self-concern. The trouble with vacations is they give us time to worry about the things we don't have time to worry about during the rest of the year. Just let the days drag a little and we overreact to our little moods; we let them get the best of us or we throw ourselves too energetically into activity to combat them.

It is wisdom to roll with the emotional punches rather than to shadowbox our psyche, but there are other lessons as well to be learned from a trip through the summer doldrums. Perhaps the first insight is to realize that these brief excursions into the grey fields of depression tell us what the experience of mental illness is like on a full-time basis for those suffering from it. We can read about it and listen to lecturers but nothing will teach us more about emotional problems than to expand on our own intermittent brushes with it. From this we can get a taste of the way the world looks day in and day out for the people who are stricken by psychological problems that sometimes seem so remote from us and so difficult to understand. A little of that kind of learning is not a dangerous thing if it enlarges our compassion and helps us to realize that individuals with emotional problems are not like creatures from another planet whose experience is totally alien to us. What they suffer is an intensified and prolonged version of the "blahs" that we quickly try to kill off with distractions and pills. It is worth a little depression now and then to achieve an insight that helps us understand and relate better to the emotionally ill. They are not so starkly different from us after all.

The next time you sail into the doldrums, don't grab for the first little blue pill around; take some soundings of your own depression, be grateful that it is not so deep after all, and make room in your understanding for those who are over their head all the time.

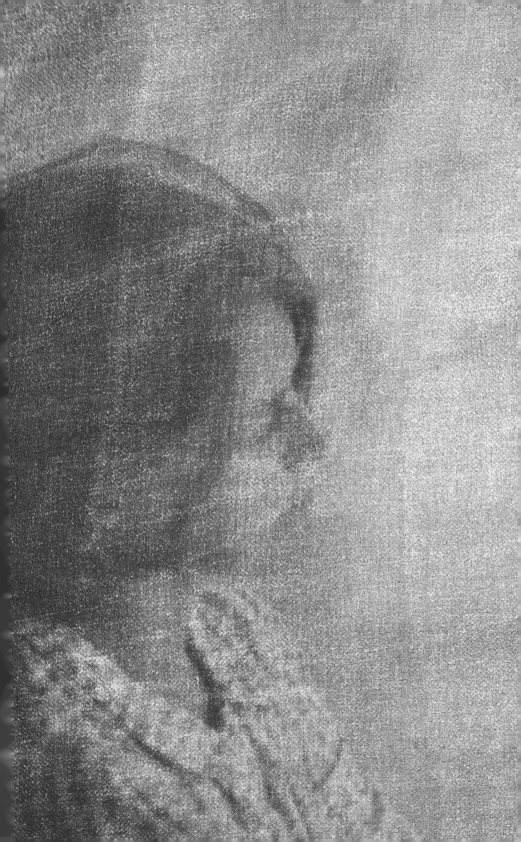

FLIGHTS OF FANTASY

NOT even the rise of the "new cinema" with all its stylized cutting and other techniques will ever surpass, for vividness and variety, the continuous showings in the private theater of fantasy within each individual's mind. Even though colorful fancies dance in the heads of the most sober looking people, few persons ever talk about them, even to themselves. What happens in their fantasy life sometimes scares them, or makes them feel guilty, or leads them to think that they are very different from everybody else. Actually, vivid fantasies are something we all have in common; they are a sign of our relationship in the human condition and they may be more helpful than they are harmful to us. We all chew on what Shakespeare called "the food of sweet and bitter fancy."

There can, however, be something terrifying and isolating about the images that flash into our heads. There is, for example, a peculiarly disturbing quality about the wild visions that arise when we cannot get to sleep or when we are awakened in the small hours of the morning. At those moments we feel all alone in the universe except for these strange imaginings that would never enter our heads in daylight. Every man has experienced this, just as every man plays the role of Walter Mitty at times. He imagines himself at the center of things, the hero who rescues the great man and then slips quietly away into the crowd without giving his name to the reporters. Yes, and every man knows that fantasies can have a strong sexual coloring which, despite the sexual revolution, still has the power to unnerve us.

Many Christians suffer a great deal because they identify sexual fantasies with the phenomenon that has been described as impure thoughts. A great deal of false guilt has arisen because of the identification of these two aspects of our mental life. Fantasies arise spontaneously, forming themselves from bits and pieces of our conscious and unconscious experience. They cannot be turned off as automatically as a TV set. As a result the man plagued with them may feel extremely guilty. Actually this experience of fantasy is quite different from some deliberate effort to generate erotic imagery. The latter is something under our control, something for which we can be responsible. The unfolding of fantasy, however, can be as endless as it is uninvited. It reflects the many layers of our human personality and is not in itself either evil or harmful.

Indeed, fantasy is the real mother of invention. The limits of man's progress, we are told, are the limits of his imagination. Even for the common man who will never conquer any new worlds, fantasy can serve a very helpful function. It allows him to test out new solutions to his problems and to explore differing roles in his responses to them. Without his imagination he could not anticipate the simplest of situations. Fantasy is also a kind of safety valve that allows us to drain off the accumulated tensions and hostilities of the day in symbolic form.

Fantasies, of course, tell us something about ourselves if we take a close look at them. Certain recurring patterns may give us a hint of what we are like deep down inside and how we really relate to other people. If we would but understand these patterns, they may give us a clue to the source of some of our frustrations and point us toward a better way of handling them.

If fantasies can help us to understand ourselves, they can also help us to understand other people. Without imagination, it would be impossible to put ourselves in the place of some other person. With the common bond of our humanity, however, and the resources of our imagination we can enter into the world of other persons and see it, as it were, from the inside. Harnessing our fantasy to this use, we can go a long way in developing our sense of compassion and in breaking down some of the emotional bases of prejudice. Imagination is a powerful vehicle for transporting ourselves into the circumstances in which others find themselves. Imagination, guided by the Christian sense of values, may be one of the most powerful weapons we can use to overcome the estrangement and loneliness that are so common in our own day.

Fantasy has its dangers and the worst of these is the failure to examine the world of our own imagination, to hold it at a distance because we are afraid of it, and to think we are different when we are really just like everybody else. The most normal people can at times have some of the wildest and most irrational fantasies. There is some comfort in understanding that we are not alone in this regard. So too there is good reason for traditional caution about not losing ourselves in a world of fantasy. One of hard-pressed man's biggest temptations is to turn away from the real world and toward a world of images and shadows. We all recognize the dreamy person who never gets his fantasies off the drawing board, the sad people who live with their private glass menageries. Sadder still are those who seek to intensify their daydreams through drugs and who take pharmaceutical trips as a substitute for real life. Sooner or later for these people the boundary between fantasy and reality becomes blurred and they easily lose their footing as well as any sure sense of themselves.

Fantasies are too common to let them be very terrifying. The average person is not trying to escape from the harshness of life through daydreaming or drugs, and most people do not try to generate erotic fantasies for their own amusement either. Men would be a little more friendly and forgiving of themselves if they recognized the very common nature of fantasy and that it can be constructive as well as harmful. Perhaps fantasy, after all, is one of those signs that this life gives us once in a while about the wonders that lie beyond all our struggles and pain, the good things that the eye has not seen and the ear has not heard and that God has waiting for us in glory.

THE WORK OF LOVE

DO you recall Sigmund Freud's famous answer to the question about man's purpose in life? "To love and to work," he said, a reply at once profound and simple. It may seem strange to associate love and work, especially to a generation whose romantic expectations run so very high. Love, however, is work, and hard work at that. It disintegrates quickly in the lives of those who do not understand this.

Love is not work in the way that digging ditches is. It would, in fact, be less exhausting if it were something quite so routine and predictable. You can dig ditches and think of something else at the same time. You cannot, however, love another person and have your mind and heart on something else at the same time. Oh, you can speak loving words, or send candy and flowers, but if your person is not really involved in a committed and consistent way, the whole thing is fake and falls apart quickly. Few things demand as much constant attention and willing effort to be fully present to another as love. Love is full of wonder and warmth and the world moving under our feet; it also demands concentration and the hard work of staying in relationship to another through all the problems and difficulties of life.

It is natural, of course, for people not to talk much about the discipline involved in loving another person responsibly. We like the bright sides of things and love is no exception. It is a terrible predicament, however, for an individual to misunderstand the dimensions of love and yet to shrink back from the hard work that is the unpublicized but full reality of love. The hard work is as simple as the effort that goes into knowing and really accepting another person once his eccentricities are exposed under the harsh light of close living. Love's labor is involved in persevering at the effort to understand another even after you think you have heard everything he has to say. The work of love is hard indeed when it demands that we overcome our tendency to turn inside ourselves when we are hurt. It is hard work to try to be vital and responsive to another when we are tired and would just as soon be left alone. Love is very demanding of the best of our energies in moments of tension and misunderstanding with those we love. We are tempted to let all that is hostile bubble up at those moments, and it is hard work to face our anger and to keep it from destroying our love.

You don't hear much about this side of love. In fact, you hear more about people who give up on trying to work out their lives together. Some of them have passed up too many chances to listen and struggle together; others are overwhelmed by the painful challenges of faithful loving. They want what can never be, that love be easy, and so they are unprepared for the reality of it. They do not even understand that embracing the painful work of loving makes it secure and solid; they do not grasp that it is in suffering the death asked of us by love that we are able to give and share more life.

One is struck, for example, by the tender reflections of the South African author Alan Paton in *For You Departed*, his memoir of his late wife. He writes with the simple openness of a man who had to face the hard work and suffering of very deep love. Paton had married a young widow who continued to wear her first wedding ring. When they had been married for some time he experienced a strong attraction to a young woman student of his. Addressing his wife in retrospect, Paton writes:

> . . . you suddenly said to me, *Are you in love with Joan?* And I said, *Yes.* You said, *What are you going to do about it?* and I said, *Stop it.* You said, *Surely, she must be consulted about it,* and I said, *We have already spoken about it.* Then I said to you, *I ask only one thing and that is to go down to Natal and say goodbye to her,* to which you replied, *I am willing that you should.* Later that day, or that night, you said to me, *What did I do wrong?* But I cannot remember what I answered, or if I answered at all. . . .

Paton went to see the girl, ended their relationship, and returned home:

> You met me at the door of the house, and you took me into your arms in that fierce way of yours, and you held back your head so that I could see the earnestness in your face, and you said to me, *I am going to make it all up to you.* I do not know when I noticed that you were no longer wearing your first wedding ring, but that

night when we went to bed it had gone from your finger. All I know is that when you died I searched the house for it. Strange, is it not, that if I found it I would have treasured it? It is a strange story altogether, isn't it? But it is a true story of life, and if I lived it again I'd like to live it the same way, only better.

This kind of facing a complicated truth together is by no means easy. Without a generous willingness born of faith in each other to work at their love the story could have gone quite differently. Similar, if less dramatic, challenges fill the calendar of every married life. Love that isn't ready to work hard at patient sharing and understanding doesn't survive these crises. For the Christian these crises are the occasions for the growth together that the Spirit gives to those who join themselves to the struggle of love. It is through the work of love that men and women discover its real meaning and it is in embracing it together that they redeem each other.

IN WHOM DO WE TRUST?

TRUST is a word that has come to be associated as much with economics as with human relationships. There are, for example, irrevocable trusts of money which, once set up, cannot be altered. But trust is better known as one of the basic ingredients of life. Man does not grow unless he receives it and he is not grown unless he can give it to others. It is an awesome and difficult aspect of life, and a dangerous one too. Unlike the special economic species, all human trust is revocable. It is not a fixed or unchanging entity anymore than life itself is. It can be taken back, it can be lost, or it can be given anew. When trust is alive it is never something static. In fact, trust really means something only when it costs something to give it. It changes people's lives when it is freely given without question or condition by those who are not afraid of the dangers of such generosity.

Trust is the quality that warms the environment of the young and grows and makes it possible for them to find their own individuality as well as their own path in life. Trust is part of the ineffable magic that can be glimpsed in the lives of people who really love each other. When they trust each other they are open and undefended, totally present to each other and, as a consequence, totally vulnerable to the hurts they may in one way or other inflict on each other. Trust is that extraordinary quality by which we make room in our lives for other people and let them see what we are really like. It is the kind of big-heartedness that allows us to see others as separate from ourselves and in need of the special freedom that trusting people grant to each other. Trust is the touch of the Spirit that casts out fear and makes it safe for other people to be themselves in our presence.

We are always looking for someone we can really trust. It is a sad thing, in a cynical world of put-ons and cop-outs where double agents have become our favorite non-heroes, to see how few people seem able to pay the price of actively trusting one another. It is far safer to protect the human heart from hurt by not trusting others. It is dangerous indeed to expose our emotions to the very special pain of abused trust. The fear of being hurt is almost an epidemic disease and so people have laid in great stores of the drugs of defensiveness. But defensiveness does not cast out fear; it doesn't even keep it at bay very well. Defensive people never feel very secure and when they withhold trust, whether in family matters or in business, they generate an interpersonal arms race deadlier than the nuclear one. Only love casts out that kind of fear, and trust is one of its essential components. It takes a lot of growing to give ourselves away in trust or to run the risk of being betrayed; it is as hard as anything man is ever likely to know. To love others enough to let them be separate rather than to control them, to be trusting even after we have been hurt—this kind of trust is very hard but essential if we really want to be givers of life to others.

Trust has many faces. It can be as simple as really trying to give our attention to a troubled person when we would rather be doing something else. If we withhold that commitment of our energies and interest we fail to trust because we present to the other only a semblance of ourselves, just enough to look interested but not enough to be touched or involved or to be hurt. And so trust is an easy thing to talk about but a hard thing to give. There are no words easier than "I trust you" even while we add silently to ourselves "but I'll keep an eye on you." So many parents say they trust their children. What they really mean is that they let the children do whatever they feel like as they pull back into their own lives because they are unable or unwilling to stay in continued relationship to the young. This is one of the breaking points of trust, the thing that tells us whether it is genuine or not. A person who really trusts another offers him support and sticks with him. He does not reassure him and then back away defensively. This emotional abandonment of others is all too common; that is why trust is all too hard to find. It is so much simpler to offer the campaign-promise kind of trust—the kind we never fully deliver until we want a new vote of confidence from others for ourselves.

Trust is not something that can be pretended. There is nothing that people see through more clearly or quickly than the shallow and superficial pseudo-trust which cuts off rather than encourages involvement with others. This is by no means restricted only to parents. You can easily see it in some of the very young who talk a good deal about trusting each other. Underneath it all, they are really saying, "Let's not demand anything of each other. Let's not take away each other's freedom." This only sounds like trust but the anxiety about not making demands tells us quickly that it is not quite the real thing. We can feel it when we are trusted and we should be able to recognize when we are challenged to trust others. Trust does take away some of our freedom, and trust keeps asking something from us long after the moment in which we have given it to someone else. The real hallmark of Christian trust is the continued concern and support we offer to others even as we keep ourselves available and vulnerable to them. Trust is an ongoing process rather than a one-time promise. It is not a yellowed document hidden in a safe-deposit box, nor an exchange of vows that grows less as we grow older. Trusting people is a Christian way of living with them on a long term basis. People who trust are genuinely rich in the things of the Spirit, and they grow more alive and richer still as they give trust away freely and fully to others.

THE HARDEST THING OF ALL FOR YOU

LIFE is so filled with hard things, misplays and misunderstandings of all kinds, that it somehow does not seem quite fair that, on top of these, we are expected to forgive others for their faults. It can't be forgiveness just in words; it has to be real or it does not work at all. Forgiveness, according to the scriptures, must come from the heart and that, of course, is exactly what makes it so hard. When we do something from our heart we are doing something with our whole person; it is the moment, if the moment is ever to be, when we make ourselves fully present to others.

Forgiveness cannot coexist with closing off some inner chambers of personality in which we can keep the fires of bitterness banked until some opportunity for revenge comes our way. But we humans like to do just that, holding on to old hurts long after everybody else but ourselves has forgotten them, warming ourselves with the knowledge that we have kept some things on file for that great getting-even day. For some of us that makes all the suffering worthwhile. We can wait, like the Count of Monte Cristo, until that moment of freedom when, blinking into the sunlight, we can take out after our enemies.

The hard part of what the Gospel says about forgiveness is that we must forgive even when we are right. Forgiveness would not make much sense any other way, of course. It is not something for those who never hurt us but for those who do. It is hard enough at times to love our friends, but the thought of forgiving our enemies is downright startling. That is what makes Christianity so different from any of the other religions that the world has ever known. It doesn't ask us simply to put up with and accept life's betrayals through some kind of sweet and quiet contemplation; it challenges us to be active, to go out and meet our enemy, not to spite him, but to embrace him. It is in the question of forgiveness that we experience down deep just how much genuine Christianity asks of us if we are sincere about following Christ closely. It is anything but easy. There is no need for any self-inflicted mortifications in the true asceticism of Christianity; just facing into the death that forgiving others demands of us is plenty. Furthermore there is a real dying to self in being able to accept the bad feelings as a part of ourselves. We like to glance over the mistakes and sticky episodes of life, not inspecting them too closely because it is too painful to do so. Self-examination comes hard especially in the situations in which we have been hurt. We do not feel much inclined to sort out the tangled feelings which are strewn across our soul like live wires.

We cannot be forgiving, however, unless we can first admit that we can be vengeful and hard of heart. We do not even experience our own personality unless we take a close look at those parts of ourselves which we would ordinarily prefer to disown. We would rather push these feelings down or hide them in a haze of forgetfulness. But then we are only trying to bury a part of ourselves. It is from that grave that ghosts arise, specters that have power only when we leave them in the darkness. Forgiveness of ourselves, it is commonly said, is necessary before we can forgive anyone else. This begins by admitting just how complex and contradictory we can sometimes be in our personal relationships. Forgiveness starts when we can recognize the fullness of our faulted selves in the human condition and not turn away. Forgiveness is accomplished when we can take responsibility for all that we are.

There is a marvelous freedom that comes to us when we have the courage to see ourselves pretty much as we are. It is this freedom that gives us the power to forgive others. And that power, of course, is none other than the power of love itself, the love that comes in life when we are truly in touch with the persons we are. Only this love enables us to redeem ourselves and others through the kind of forgiveness that is tempered in the cleansing fires of self-examination and self-acceptance. For most of us this kind of forgiveness remains an ideal that we work towards throughout all our days. The pursuit of the fullness of forgiveness of ourselves and others is one of the signs that we are living and growing in the Spirit. When we can forgive ourselves for the fact that it is necessary for us to keep working at this virtue, we will have taken a big step closer to achieving it.

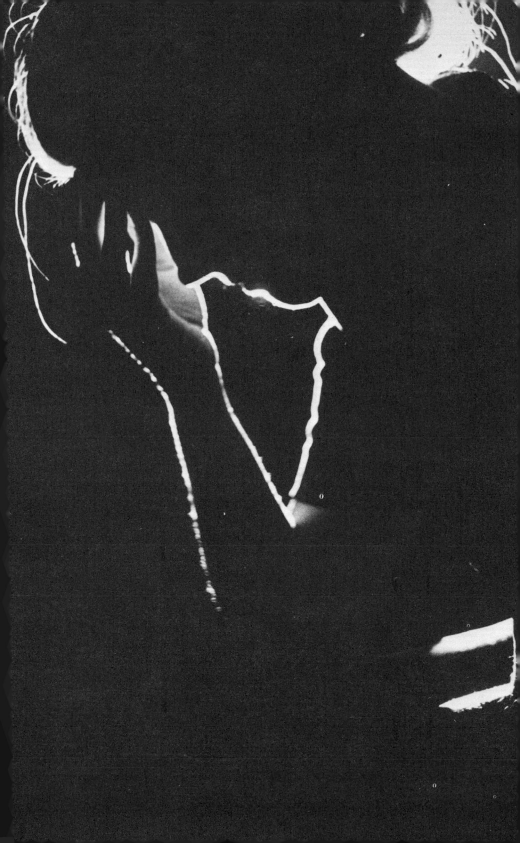

THE MISTAKE-MAKERS

IF there is anything worse than making a mistake, the cynics say, it is getting caught at it. From the first time we were discovered putting our hand into a forbidden cookie jar to the last time we felt that sudden shock at seeing the state trooper in our rearview mirror, we know the experience well. We do not enjoy, and tend to suppress, insofar as it is possible, those moments in which our indiscretion, bad judgment, or even simple human foibles are uncovered.

It is very hard to integrate our mistakes into our lives. We tend to disown them, to look the other way, and we certainly don't like to learn from them. If we did, we wouldn't keep making the same mistakes over and over again. There is something embarrassing, something deeply shaming in the uneasiness we can feel in our very bones when we have committed a blunder. We do not like to admit it to ourselves because we might have to take a long hard look at it, acknowledge the failure as something that came from us and not from some mysterious source, and go on living as best we can. We don't like to make mistakes and yet we do it all the time. It is the stickiness of trying to unravel why we made the mistake, or continue to make the mistake, that is frequently the most difficult part of the whole thing.

We often get caught quite innocently, or so it seems, in the crossfire of events that show up our imperfections and inconsistencies. There are some situations, for example, in which it is hard not to make a mistake. Such is the situation when we find ourselves under pressure from two friends who happen for the moment to be enemies of each other. Even in trying to help them heal their wounds, it is difficult not to step on some sensitive nerve endings. We sometimes despair of peacemaking altogether. And all too often the people involved end up mad at us rather than at each other. It is impossible to avoid such situations except through disappearing or falling off the face of the earth. The latter is the maneuver of choice when we try to do good and end up doing badly.

We don't, however, have to be innocent mediators to find ourselves mistake-prone. There is something in us that leads us, on certain occasions at least, to say the wrong thing, to laugh at the wrong moment, or doze off when we should be alert. Making mistakes is really a part of every day's experience. It is no wonder that we prefer to remember the happy events of life and that we have such powerful psychological mechanisms to blot out the things that are embarrassing. "Blessed are the forgetful," Nietzsche once wrote, "for they get the better even of their blunders." But it is not easy to forget our mistakes, or to live them down, and sometimes our regrets get so heavy that they weigh us down and keep us from pursuing life as freely as we should.

If we stand back, however, and take a good look at man we realize that he is, above almost everything else, a mistake-maker. We can recognize the feelings of embarrassment and uneasiness that go along with errors because we have all committed them so often. We are brothers in not learning from our mistakes precisely because we don't feel like performing post-mortems on them. We would rather just let them be buried and forgotten. It takes a genius, James Joyce wrote in *Ulysses,* to get through life without mistakes. But that is because the genius can turn his errors into what Joyce calls "the portals of discovery."

Not many of us are able so to romanticize our errors. The best thing for us, then, is to approach ourselves with a little more understanding and a greater willingness to accept our imperfect state. Indeed, it is the fear of making a mistake that paralyzes some people so that they never use their talents very much in life at all. Not liking flaws in their performance they hold back waiting for that moment or that time in life when they will get this down perfectly, whether it is speaking a foreign language, teaching a class, or giving a speech. At that far dawn, no one will be able to laugh at them and they will not feel that fast spreading chill that the veteran mistake-maker knows so well. But that perfect day never does come. In the meanwhile many people postpone getting into life until it is really too late. Then nobody cares whether they make mistakes or not anymore. The saddest graveyard is not that one in which our mistakes are buried but the one in which the talents of people who are afraid to make mistakes rest undisturbed.

Mistakes seem increasingly intolerable in the age of machines which are supposed to run so smoothly. I could not help but think of this after reading the scientific discussion in which so many eminent men expressed concern about the scientific mistakes of the latest visit of men to the moon. The rockets performed perfectly, the trajectories unfolding quite in accord with the mathematics that dictated them. The flight plan was a masterpiece of cool calculation. However, the scientists experienced disappointment because the astronauts were men quite thrilled by being on the moon. Their vital exuberance led them, among other things, to ruin a television camera and to leave a large set of pictures behind when they took off. Men were dancing on the moon, responding to something deeply human, manifesting the wonderful unpredictability of mistake-making man. The mistakes were, I think, worth it just to hear the sound of men laughing on the moon's surface. It gives all the rest of us mistake-makers heart. Perhaps we can recognize our common-flawed humanity as we see men involved in such cosmic playfulness. We are mistake-makers, we always will be, and the sooner we are able to forgive ourselves for it, the richer will be our enjoyment of life.

A CLEVER PLAN BUT
IT WON'T WORK (I DON'T THINK)

DID you ever get the funny feeling at a meeting, or perhaps in a private discussion, that, despite all the talk, somebody, somehow or other, was managing not to get to the point? It is a strange experience for the direct and the sincere to find that the small sandbar of reason on which they are standing is slowly being worn away by a heavy tide of hogwash. At first it is hard to believe that a discussion, ostensibly called for a sane and useful objective, should be so deliberately and obviously frustrated. But it happens time and again in settings as varied as the Senate floor and your living room. Suddenly the least important subject gets extensive discussion, the clock runs out, and the serious question that brought everybody together in the first place never gets discussed at all. Why does it happen and what do you do when it happens to you?

Maybe we should review some examples. Did you ever attend a faculty meeting to talk about something important only to suffer through two hours about professors' parking regulations? Did you ever have some friend, desperation edging his voice, call you over at a late hour only to beat around the bush aimlessly after you arrive? Car salesmen, who are almost as good as native Irishmen at not answering direct questions, have mastered completely the art of talking about something else when you are trying to find out what it is really going to cost you to get that new car. After many years they build a certain intimidation into their manner that makes the customer feel slightly apologetic for taking their time in the first place. Nobody, of course, beats the Irish who, the legends tell us, learned circumlocution during the bad days when the English were always bearing down on them for this reason or that. We have all heard of the Irishman giving directions to the lost traveler. "If you want to get to Dublin," he says charmingly, "then it would be better to start from some place else." A friend of mine, worn out from trying to extract a yes or no from an Irishman, thought he had one cornered outside a post office. "Is that the post office?" he asked, sure that the answer would have to be short and to the point. But this was no challenge at all to the Irishman who replied, "Is it a stamp you want?"

But what do you do when you cannot seem to get anybody to come to the point, when you feel one more moment of this kind of delay and you will surrender to unconsciousness? If you get angry you fall into the trap to which such roundabout conversations very often lead. You are then the one who breaks up the meeting, who makes it impossible for anything to be accomplished; it is you, who seems all innocence, who is the villain. And it isn't very helpful to get up and leave, to heave an inkwell through a window, or to throw a punch at the man sitting on your left. That is the kind of fantasy this frustration induces in the normally calm and collected person who wants to find out only why the discussion or the meeting is not really getting anywhere.

One must turn to another level of speculation, the one a floor or so below the surface of events, where we are able to discover the explanation for why things are moving sideways instead of forward. Often enough, if it is a meeting, the issues have already been settled outside of it and nobody wants to discuss anything important because there is no point to it. More often, however, the true problem is just too much for the people to deal with, even though they know perfectly well what it is. It is too much because they are the people responsible for dealing with it, and they cannot summon up the strength to respond. It is much better, then, to discuss some problem they can deal with, howsoever petty, rather than one they cannot deal with, howsoever real. All the distracting talk is a psychological camouflage that keeps you away from the important topic, but also tells you quite clearly that, for some reason or other, this individual or this group is incapable of dealing with it at the moment.

There is not much percentage in trying to force the issue rationally because the actual obstacles are on the emotional level. Until these are dealt with there will be no progress made anyway. You only get more frustrated if you persist in trying to discuss what others are emotionally unprepared to talk about. The average person does not find it easy to help others identify the emotional blocks that make them avoid the point of discussion, even though in the long run this is the very thing they must come to terms with. Better to save your breath or use your intelligence to try to fathom the level that tells you what is really happening, or rather, why nothing is happening at all. But do not try to apply reason. As the Irishman said, if you want to get to the point, it's better to start from some place else.

ON UNDERSTANDING UNDERSTANDING

UNDERSTANDING is as necessary for our human survival as fresh air and food are for our physical survival. But understanding is itself often misunderstood. This is done, for example, by those who believe that to be understanding towards someone we must necessarily agree with him. Perhaps this is because it is really much easier to agree with a person (and we all know the many situations in life where our friends press us keenly for some endorsement of their position) than it is to enter into their world and see things as if we were looking through their eyes. To understand another, however, means that we put aside evaluating him for a moment, that we check our readiness to judge the other as right or wrong. To be understanding we do not have to be that wise. What we must do is listen carefully and look deeply to catch what the other person, whether spouse, friend, or temporary adversary, is trying to tell us. That is not an easy task at all because it demands that we give up being spectators and judges and that we engage ourselves in sensing everything the other person, through words, gestures, and even signs, struggles to say. No wonder some people prefer to offer a dangerously surface-like agreement: "Sure, sure," a clap on the back and a quick self-extraction from a difficult situation. Lots of life goes on like that, and too much of it between people who really owe understanding to each other. To understand somebody else, we must make ourselves as fully present as possible to them without trespassing heedlessly into their inner selves. This demands attention and interest but not agreement; indeed, to agree or to disagree hurriedly would distort or destroy both the effort and effects of understanding. Lesson one, then, in taking a look at understanding tells us to examine our own need to agree or disagree with others and to learn how to take this into account the next time we really want to understand someone.

The person who makes an effort to understand the complexities of life knows that it is hard work. It is important, then, that he invest his energy in understanding the right aspect of human troubles. Sometimes we emphasize the problem rather than the person who has the problem, and this is to put the wrong thing into focus altogether. There are no such things as problems that enjoy an existence separate from the people who experience them. To analyze the problem as if it could be objectified independently of the human figures involved may allow us to make sure and accurate calculations about its dimensions, but, in omitting the people, we automatically misunderstand the situation.

Nevertheless, it is easier to get all the facts, as, for example, we might do with a son or a student who wants to change his major in college. You can total up the credits he has gained already, examine his grade point average, list all the courses he has taken, and check off all the specifications of the various life careers from which he must make a choice. On paper, a strong case can be made one way or another depending on how these all appear when they are seen in black and white. We have, we might say, understood the problem, because we have taken all its elements into account. All, of course, but the person who must make the choice, the individual whose mixed feelings and uncertain aspirations still make it difficult for him to decide. Simply making the problem clearer may not help him at all. He is the one who needs the understanding; one must bring him and his reactions into the picture or there is really no understanding of the total situation at all. And, unless the individual who has the problem is understood, it is difficult to be of any really effective help to him.

Probably the classic example of misapplied understanding was the space scientist at Cape Kennedy whose wife complained about his long hours and her disrupted home life. He immediately turned to his sliderule and worked out a new hour by hour domestic schedule for her. He had measured a problem, but because he misunderstood his own wife and her symbolic cry for more human and less scientific attention from him, he made things worse by his proposed solution.

Understanding is not for things or abstract ideas when we are dealing with anxious humans. Get the worried person and his or her feelings about the problem into perspective and you have come a long way toward genuine understanding.

Another important factor in getting better at understanding others is learning how to listen. Lots of people have an idea that this is what they should do. It is, after all, one of the most common demands in everyday experience ("Won't you just listen to me for a minute?") and in the pop psychology explanations of just about everything ("The older generation must learn to listen more to the voices of youth").

The problem arises because, even with all the good will in the world, it is difficult for people to listen correctly. Listening is an active, not a passive process. It is not enough to sit there, our thousand-mile-away thoughts masked by an interested look. You really do not hear anything that way and, of course, you do not really understand anything that way. Faking it doesn't work; in fact, as one might suspect, it is destructive of real understanding.

Others are baffled about the active process of listening because they concentrate on the wrong things. It is quite possible for a person to say, "I have listened to every word you have said but I still don't understand what you are trying to tell me." That is because understanding is not really directed at the words, or the content, of what another says; it is directed rather to the inner motivation for the words they choose to speak, to the message of their feelings which they are struggling to put into language for us. All the illustrations and examples that a person gives us are merely part of the effort to share their emotional reactions to some event or some conflict; every gesture and inflection is part of the total effort to get something inside of them on the outside. Here again, in other words, our understanding is not directed to the words, the phrases, or the examples, as much as to the whole person of the individual who is speaking to us. As a wise man once put it, an active listener shifts from "hearing *what* the other says" to "hearing what *the other* says." Probably the most helpful question to put to ourselves when we are trying to understand somebody else is: "What is this person feeling in order to say this to me?" In the answer to that question we begin to discover the real message and to understand the person who is trying to share it with us.

Obviously, concentration is necessary to sense correctly the message which the other person attempts to convey, for it is sometimes wrapped in confused language. We have to start hearing the language of emotion rather than just the language of intellect. To hear this, we must, as a famous psychiatrist once said, begin "listening with the third ear." There is another aspect to this powerful form of understanding. We must heighten our sensitivity not only to what is going on inside the other but also to what is going on inside ourselves. Unless we can hear and understand what is happening in our own reactions, we may not hear the other very well at all. Our own feelings, often subtly defended against, can be a form of static that cuts off our reception of what the other has to say.

For example, our own needs may play a major role in how understanding we can really be. If we have a need always to be right, then we may find it very difficult to listen without inner opposition or disagreement on our part. Something they say about politics or Church renewal or the peace movement may challenge a conviction of our own and cause us to react defensively. Understanding is not forwarded when our own reactions lead us to correct the other, or to get into an argument with him.

Our own feelings need not lead us into disagreement with the other, of course. Sometimes, the opposite may be true. We so approve of some attitude of the other that we begin to use him to validate our own outlook; we reverse roles so that we end up, quite unconsciously at times, looking for understanding from him. A wide range of inner feelings can interfere with our really hearing the other person. We can let our own anxieties dominate us so that we catch only a fraction of what he says; sometimes we can let our own thoughts wander to such an extent that we are hardly present to the other individual at all. At times, we feel so sure we know what he is going to say that we hardly make the effort (and a constant effort is needed) to listen to him at all.

The person who would be truly understanding must deal with his own inner self, realizing the importance of his own reactions, and sensitively taking them into account so that they do not destroy his efforts to listen carefully. There is a Christian note to the process to which we must give ourselves when we want to understand. In a real sense, we have to empty ourselves of our own concerns, die to our distractions, and control our own needs, if we are to be as fully present as possible in understanding the other. The redemptive sequence is reproduced wherever and whenever one person takes the time and makes the effort to be understanding. He must first come alive, be truly incarnate if you will, in relationship to the other. Then he must be ready to die to himself and to all the interference that arises within himself, interference which can so hamper understanding. A real communication of understanding is crowned with resurrection, as we give new life to the other and, at the same time, gain fuller life for ourselves.

THE POST-DECISION BLUES

PART of our folklore tells us that we will feel better once we have made a decision about some important event in our life. "The worst is over once the decision is made," the sage will tell us— whether what we decided has to do with our major in college, our partner for life, or our job for the time being. After having weighed the alternatives and panned out the sand of our whims from the gold dust of our real motivations, we finally say this is it, this is the long-deferred moment of truth, the point where we finally commit ourselves one way or the other. That should settle it, we feel, and so it does for many of the decisions we make in life. But there are other choices, with some of life's most important among them, that won't stay put; they keep wiggling in our consciousness, nagging at us now and then, and sometimes even presenting themselves once again for a renewed decision.

The effect of finding a decision coming back for re-examination after we thought it had been filed away for good is disconcerting and even depressing. Did we think it over enough, we ask ourselves. Did we really take enough time with it? Only the wisest and most philosophical are immune from this kind of self-doubt, because they have learned that no choice is ever perfect, and they can live completely with that knowledge. The average person is more vulnerable to wondering about his choices, and at times it is a fine line between that and regrets.

Psychology, however, has discovered certain things about our decision-making processes, and a little knowledge of these can be a big help in handling the inner questioning that may persist after a big decision is made. For example, there is a systematic tendency in all of us to begin to perceive more clearly the positive aspects of the alternatives we have rejected as soon as we have rejected them. It is a sort of over-the-shoulder-the-grass-is-greener syndrome. The person who buys house A, which is close to his work and has low maintenance costs, suddenly sees far more clearly the advantages of houses B and C which are freer of noise and air pollution, closer to resort areas, and near the new super-highway they just announced they are building out that way next year. At the same time you begin to see more clearly the problems connected with the decision you have made—the new lawn you have to put in, the higher property tax, etc. This combination of awareness can lead a man to sleepless nights, not because he has really made a wrong decision, but because he sees the advantage-disadvantage quotient in a light that was unavailable to him before he made his choice. In other words, the act of choice itself has this effect on us. And we should not be surprised by it. Better, in fact, to anticipate this and be ready to take it into account rather than succumb to the distorted impression that you made a mistake. For you will not be able to judge that accurately anyway until your time and distance perspective is much greater.

Some of our major commitments thrust themselves up out of the sea of our consciousness like the Loch Ness monster from time to time and we are not sure whether the phenomenon is real or not. In strange and vagrant moments we find ourselves with the decision wide open before us again: Do I really want to go on loving this person? Do I really want to be a teacher anymore? Do I want to continue as a priest? Do I want to confirm the choice I made once, long ago it seems, when I was a slightly different sort of person? This kind of internal question presents itself regularly around the issues which are most important to us in life. The man who denies that he has ever had these kinds of thoughts has just never bothered to listen to himself very carefully. For the big things ask us to choose them again, not to generate regrets in us, but to seek affirmation of ourselves in the deepest relationships of our lives. It is the nature of love, work and friendship to be open to our every new response rather than closed off as though they were not really a living part of us. "Once and for all;" "Till death do us part;" and "Now and forever"—these are some of our most profound phrases but they take on their significance because they refer to relationships which, by their nature, demand that we keep saying yes to them as the years go by. It would be a strange relationship indeed, and not much of a one at that, which did not demand reaffirmation from us now and then. Birthdays, anniversaries and other ceremonials are man's way of setting up occasions to underscore his life decisions all over again. So man goes through his life, always ready to pull at the threads that forever hang loose from the choices he has made. But he would be less depressed by the imperfection of his decision-making if he realized it was common and, in the most important parts of his life, a good thing besides.

INTIMACY AND EMOTIONAL INVOLVEMENT

HALF the people around us speak about the need to get involved while the other half are preoccupied with getting uninvolved. This is especially true in our emotional lives. Men long for closeness but their fear of it draws them to the shady coolness of non-involvement. Coolness is an antidote for the heat of emotional involvement which can soar like a fever in close personal relationships. There is not much in life without closeness to others, and there is no closeness without the challenge of intimacy.

Some people become deliberately involved at every emotional opportunity; others get involved innocently, but their innocence is soon erased by the frictions of being close to other persons. These are the terrible problems that go along with caring about other people and what happens to them. It is an inevitable hazard of first love, but a danger also for parents and teachers who are supposed to know better, an experience so common that almost everyone can still feel the twinges of pain in emotional wounds that they thought had long since healed. How, these people ask, shaking themselves free for the moment from the sleepless nights and the gnawing preoccupations of emotional involvement, can something so good seem to be so bad?

These reflections describe over-involvement, of course, and that is the prime hazard of any kind of involvement at all. How does one draw the line, or know when things are getting too complex, or when to stay at a slightly restrained distance? The difficulty is that when men do not have immediate answers to these deep questions of life a certain defensiveness of adjustment creeps into their behavior. "I'll never let that happen to me again," the man says, remembering still the pain of giving his heart away too freely to a woman who, as it turned out, never took him as seriously as he thought. Even first friendships, those tentative probings of the depths of another, generate pain along with wonder. "Keep your distance" is a rule of thumb for emotional survival for those who have been disappointed in friendship or love.

It is hardly any wonder that the model of the so-called professional or objective relationship becomes the option for many. This permits people to stay at a convenient distance from others, with the thermostat of their emotions set in the cool but comfortable range. This latter adjustment is very popular today because, if we are cool, our defense is the pretense that we do not care and never will care enough to let another person hurt us. We can, after all, do without being close to others; we can keep our hearts secure by being above it all. I cannot help but think of the woman who chose in her marriage to be childless because, as she put it, if she had no one to hope in, she would never be disappointed.

And yet no one can really do without others, not for very long anyway. The ability to enter into intimacy with another person is both the seal and the source of our maturity. This kind of intimacy goes beyond although it includes sexual intimacy. It means living and sharing close up to each other, so close that we must be ourselves in relationship to each other or we are really nothing. And everything we learn about relationships in psychology reaffirms what Christianity has known so well: sharing what is real about ourselves with others is what gives all the light and warmth to life itself. Psychological jargon has stylized but not really invented the interpersonal realm that describes, as well as anything, what life is all about. This is the whole mystery of being present to each other with as little pretense as possible.

The great wonder of life is that we are not alone, that we can and must make a difference to each other in as personal a way as possible. We are called, all of us, to be friends, not just on good days or when the fancy or our own need strikes us, but on the bleak bad days when even the birds have nothing to sing about. The Christian life commits us to a journey, and only love makes us forget the lack of signposts and the long stretches of unpaved roads. The journey is possible only because on it we find not just each other but an understanding of the values of life that we can learn only in each other's presence. That is the mystery of intimacy, the lifebase of all true lovers in their growth together in the Spirit.

Intimacy of this kind demands involvement but, twice shy because of painful involvements, we may decide that the journey of life must be made cautiously and self-protectively. The world does not lack people who settle for a life adjustment in which they won't be hurt. They are really defending against over-involvement, giving up because the task of working through the challenge of intimacy seems too much for them. But working through what it means to be in love with another person is what marriage is all about. This is realized, however, only after the dizzying fantasies about love that are so common today are put aside. Romance has become a holy grail; many dream that they can achieve it without any risk to themselves. It is small wonder that people are so easily confused and so easily discouraged when the course of love does not run at all smoothly.

Over-involvement is an excess of the immature, an over-investment that is made by those who do not really understand themselves and who dangerously overextend the resources of their personality before they have really put it together for themselves. There are pains enough in all loving, even for the most mature of us; there is an almost crippling kind of suffering for those who enter a relationship in search of their own identity. Our identity is something we must bring to our relationships and, while we will deepen our understanding of ourselves through friendship and love, we court broken hearts if we enter relationships in order to find out who we are.

The first lesson to be learned about intimacy and emotional involvement centers on examining our own needs. It is hard to do this but there is no learning the lessons of involvement if we fail to do it. Very often the biggest hurts, the ones that make us set up the highest defenses, arise precisely because we have responded to our own needs more than to the other person. We have wanted them to like us, to respond to us, more than we have wanted to love them. Unless we can get our own needs into focus we can only claw and hurt both our own heart and the hearts of others in the close quarters of friendship and love. The Spirit touches us when we give as well as take, when we can let other people preserve their individuality and preserve our own even in the midst of love. Authentic involvement means meeting the other as he or she truly is rather than as a projection of our own needs and daydreams. When we join what is true in another with what is true in ourselves, then the involvement that is essential to intimacy takes healthy root.

If we do not bring some measure of our own identity, and some appreciation of the identity of the other to our relationship, then we are inviting the suffering we call overinvolvement.

THOSE HOLIDAY BLUES

SOME of man's darkest hours black out the skies he feels should be the brightest. For example, nothing eats at the heart of a man more than the depression that can suddenly overcome him during the holiday season. Even when he has experienced the holiday blues before and tries to keep on guard against them, he can find himself surprised and pushed by them into what seems a bottomless pit. All he knows is that he is falling, that there are no handholds around, and that it will be a relief to hit bottom. It is that long slow fall into the depths that turns a holiday season into a melancholy time and makes a dirge out of the music of celebration.

This is a common problem around Christmas time, especially during the letdown that inevitably comes after hard work at trying to make Christmas merry for everyone else. It may strike the father who has just assembled what seemed to be a thousand toys for the children he loves. Instead of being able to relish their enjoyment of them, he finds himself suddenly tired and depressed, as though a gauzy film of melancholy had dropped between him and his family. It can strike the wife, who having spent herself in getting everything ready for a good time, finds that she feels empty and unenthusiastic when she should be enjoying herself. These depressions would be more understandable if one could point to something as simple and direct as the cost of Christmas shopping. They are not, however, related to the impending arrival of bills. Neither are they attached to illness of a physical kind, nor to some clear emotional disappointment. The holiday blues seem to settle on healthy people who cannot easily identify the reason for their sudden shift in mood.

It is probably reassuring to know that many people experience this kind of depression and that it is not strange or unusual to find it in one's life. It seems to come quite regularly for people when there has been a lot of physical and emotional energy expended. It seems to be part of the strange feelings of anticlimax that human beings so often experience when they have looked forward to something with great anticipation. The event comes off and they go down, deflated it would almost seem by the sudden relaxation of the tension that goes with achieving some goal.

So many weeks or hours are pointed toward this occasion that the letdown can be severely discouraging. It is made the more so in contrast to the general festivity of the season and our own inner expectations that we should feel better than we do. Probably the best immediate antidote for the holiday blues is not another cup of eggnog but a frank admission of the way we really feel. We sometimes redeem ourselves when we can stop demanding that we feel differently than we do and can accept the fact that, in the flawed human state, ups and downs are as natural as the sunrise. I am not suggesting that we give in to the blues and thereby cause the disease to spread to those closest to us. It is helpful, however, to acknowledge our shift in mood and to examine it briefly to see if we cannot understand a little better the course of events that has brought it about. In that way, we possess ourselves more fully because we honestly face the state in which we find ourselves. Much better to do this than to try to hide our depression with alcohol, increased activity, or just a retreat into growling bad temper. The holiday blues always tempt us to let the scrooge out of ourselves, but this is very unfair to those around us; and at holiday time, those around us are the ones we love most and are the ones we can hurt most easily when we don't try to respond positively to the syndrome of holiday depression.

In any case, the holiday blues do not mean that a man is neurotic. They mean rather that he is normal, that he is subject to the kind of swings in feeling that are common to all human beings, and that he would do well to face them directly and truthfully. Perhaps we can give each other an added Christmas gift by vowing at least not to infect each other if the holiday blues settle on us. That might be one small step for us but a giant leap for our family and friends.

NEVER IS A BIG WORD

IN preparing some notes for a new book recently, I was intrigued by the Jerusalem Bible translation of Paul's famous paragraphs on love in his letter to the Corinthians. The translation reads, "Love is *never* jealous. . . . it is *never* rude or selfish. . . ." The more I thought about it the less I believed that Paul, scarred by shipwreck, courtroom appearances and inconstant friends, could have used the adverb *never*. *Never* seemed an especially inappropriate word. It is a qualifier with too little give in it for anybody who has ever known love in everyday life. *Never*, like *always*, is a big word, one that may safely be used when referring to angels or statues, which are changeless because they are not alive. It is, however, a dangerously inaccurate word to employ in reference to such a restless and shifting creature as man. *Never*, *always* and other absolutes are the kind of words people use in their New Year's resolutions. They have a built-in fragility which causes them to shatter quickly in ice-cold January. "Never say never," Harry Truman once said, "because never is a hell of a long time." Indeed, most of us know how big a word *never* is from some experience of our own fallibility.

People find out, for example, that they frequently end up doing the things they said they would *never* do, whether this concerns where they live, the work they do or even eating again the thing that makes them sick. And people find that it is very difficult to do the things they say they will *always* do. Man is made in the human condition more for exceptions than for a letter-perfect keeping of inflexible resolutions.

That is why it is misleading to say that love is *never* this, or is *always* that. This is not to excuse the human defects or the faults that make it hard to apply these words to the life of man. It is, however, to recognize that the Spirit of Love operates in the human condition where there are gaps in the best of lives and where our scars show that we heal incompletely from the wounds of living. When you say *never* you eliminate any margin for error.

The Christian life, however, has wide margins and unlimited forgiveness for those who fall off center now and then. Of its very essence Christian love tolerates mistakes and failures; its most incredible strength is that it bridges gaps and that it pulls the flawed material of life gently together again. Love, if it is anything, is the power the Spirit gives us to respond in the human situation where we are always falling short or not quite measuring up. Love links people in the constantly shifting experience of life in which they can hurt and disappoint each other even after they have said, "I'll *never* hurt you again," or "I'll *always* be kind and gentle."

Lovers make mistakes all the time and constantly sense the tremors of their own shortcomings even as they try their best to overcome them. The ideal of Christian love is not one of rigid perfection, free of all blemishes and unseemly thoughts. The miracle of Christian love is that it is a gift to sinners who can actively accept each other as less than perfect and who thereby redeem each other continually. They keep reaching out, they keep trying to understand, and they keep growing together at the same time.

People who love each other recognize the tension that accompanies their imperfection. They know that they are not immune to anger, or the pull of other attractions, or the feeling of suddenly being distant from one another. What love does is enable them to handle all these common experiences of life and to integrate them without letting them infect and destroy their life together. Love lets people face conflict, even competition at times, without making every situation of stress a battle to the death. Through the power of love people are able to cope with the difficulties of life and achieve a new and higher ground of maturity together. The great thing about love is that it is made for and found only among ordinary, mistake-making people.

Sin may consist in the refusal to be redemptive in the human condition. Its true face may be seen only when people give up on each other, letting life fall apart because they will not love enough to pull it back together again. The worst sin of all is to disdain the human condition, to turn away from the demands of love, and to not care anymore. This is indeed to sin against the Spirit. Sin is a terrible estrangement from the human setting, a rejection of the simple tasks of reconciliation and forgiveness, a refusal to love enough to make each other whole.

Christianity says that there is hope, even for mankind so weighed down with a consciousness of everything it can do wrong. This hope springs from the saving power of love that is stronger than the faults of men. One thinks of Martin Buber's translation of the Hasidic parable:

> (He) sat among peasants in a village inn and listened to their conversation. Then he heard how one asked the other, "Do you love me?" And the latter answered, "Now, of course, I love you very much." But the first regarded him sadly and reproached him for such words: "How can you say you love me? Do you know, then, my faults?" And then the other fell silent, and silent they sat facing each other, for there was nothing more to say. He who truly loves knows, from the depths of his identity with the other, from the root ground of the other's being he knows where his friend is wanting. This alone is love. (*I and Thou*, p. 248)

The Spirit makes it possible for lovers who have wounded each other to bring again a healing to one another. It means that we can make up for our smallness, our jealousies, and all our broken resolutions, not by a new and unrealistic pledge never to fall again, but by a willingness to take up the task of loving again. Real love begins when we are ready to forgive one another and to help each other to do better the next time, not when we expect each other to go through life with all our lines letter perfect. Christian love is not perfect because it is always growing. The life of the Spirit is only an approximation of *never* and *always*, and its glory is revealed in the life to the full that it makes available for everyman.

P.S. Scripture scholars tell me that St. Paul didn't really mean *never* anyway.

WHAT AM I GETTING
OUT OF THIS ANYWAY?

MAN is proud of his progress through history, proud, for example, of the things that couldn't be done but which he ended up doing anyway. He is also puzzled by the fact that, while he seems to want to move forward against the odds, he can also slide backwards against his best interests and instincts. Men have wrung their hands and pounded their heads in regret at the wrong directions they have taken and which, strangely enough, they often end up taking over again. Experience, they say, is the best teacher, but men frequently do not learn from it as they go on repeating the same mistakes in their personal and public lives season after season.

A long list would not exhaust the examples of the perilous and self-defeating positions into which men constantly place themselves. "Whatever you have, spend less," Samuel Johnson once urged, but many men find it almost necessary to do just the opposite. The resulting worry, the ulcers and the slow contamination of the relationships they prize most do not seem enough to keep them from the temptations of buying on credit. Then there are those people, found in families, businesses and even monasteries, who relate to each other by fighting constantly. They are always upset and they are always irritated, but they seem incapable of finding any other way of getting along.

The same is true of men and women who keep separating and coming back together again, missing each other when they are apart but knocking each other's brains out when they get together. Add to the list those who keep doing things that get them into serious trouble even when they know full well what will happen to them because of it. The man who always comes late to work or who always drinks just a little more than is good for him; the man who complicates his already painful present by postponing important obligations to an indefinite future—these are the snags on which supposedly progressive man keeps catching himself. How does it all fit together and make any sense at all? Are these just random and unexplainable aspects of human nature?

The reasons we do what we do can be very complex, but there are always reasons. Man's behavior does not come out of nowhere and, with patience and insight, it can be traced down to its origins even when these are deep in his unconscious life. Indeed, the examples given may be the iceberg towers floating on the sea of the unconscious, signs of how much more there is below than above the surface. Obviously, very tangled and complex motivation cannot be unraveled by the amateur psychologist, no matter how good willed he may be. Obviously, many people need professional help in order to get to the real roots of the things which they do to defeat themselves in daily life.

On the other hand, even reasonably mature and healthy people are frequently puzzled by why they do things which they know will hurt either themselves or other people. With a little reflection, or perhaps the ready ear of a good friend, they can achieve a better understanding of their behavior. They may come to see it in clearer perspective and to avoid the mistake in the future. I think one of the most helpful questions a person can ask when he is mystified by his own moods or actions is this: "What am I getting out of this anyway?" This question is helpful because we really do not do anything that does not reward us in one way or another. The reward need not be very obvious to be effective. It is just that we do not often inspect the dynamics of our day-to-day life and so we fail to appreciate the nature of many of the psychological transactions which we carry out with ourselves. When our behavior causes us pain or embarrassment, a close look within oneself may reveal that we are balancing the psychological books by punishing ourselves in some disguised way for something about which we feel guilty deep down inside. So too, we may discover that we endure certain punishing behavior, something as simple as drinking tonight even though we know we will be desperately ill tomorrow, because we want to seize the short term gain, the comforting escape through alcohol, so that we do not have to look at the picture of our long-term responsibilities.

This question helps because it can give us a clue about some pattern of our behavior to which we would otherwise be quite insensitive. It helps us to achieve the self-knowledge which is so hard to get at and which is indispensable for further steps toward maturity. The answer to the question about what we are getting out of a certain form of behavior leads us to ask other questions which can bring us into corners of our personality which are strongly influential but from which we have shielded ourselves. All our behavior, however, hangs together; it is part of the mystery and wonder of the human condition. When a man wants to see himself whole, to see his actions as a language that can lead him to a new understanding of himself, then he might well begin, the next time he is puzzled by some self-inflicted psychological reversal, by asking, "What am I getting out of this anyway?"

DID YOU EVER FEEL LIKE CRYING?

TEARS say a lot but sometimes they are hard to understand. We can weep for joy just as we weep for sorrow; some people weep at almost anything while others hardly ever weep at all. Tears are a language that everybody speaks, but with different accents and meanings according to the complicated laws of how we have learned to express our emotions. The French, they say, cry quite freely while Americans shed private tears to express something very deep in their lives. How can something so wrenching to the soul be described as "having a *good* cry"?

The truth is, of course, that we have all felt like crying and we know from experience that it can have many meanings. Tears can be the recourse of children who are on the spot—the defense against adult questioning or accusation which wins them mercy rather than justice in the small missteps of childhood. These are the tears that must be put away if a person is to move into maturity. Sadly enough, there are those who go on weeping the defensive tears of childhood for the rest of their lives whenever they are in difficult circumstances. These people never understand grown-up tears, the tears that are much more than the sobs of self-pity. Oh, we can all feel sorry for ourselves at times but if we are relatively mature we can catch our emotions and save ourselves and others from the self-indulgent tears we might otherwise shed.

Tears in the mature person's life come at very deep moments of sadness and joy, on occasions of separation and reunion, whenever love shows through in life. Tears are above all a sign that we are alive, that the heart still beats because we care about someone or something enough to cry. Only the dead or the totally despairing have no tears. People who live with hope and trust can cry aloud; they are alive and have known the meaning of love.

Some men hide their tears to show their strength; others keep their sorrow secret because weeping seems a source of shame for them; and heavy hearted are those whose eyes are dry because their wound is so deep that they cannot let the hurt out at all. The loneliest of men are those who have no one in whose presence they feel free to weep, no one whose responding love can redeem them from the sadness that has settled into their souls.

It is a hard thing to cry but it is not a bad thing. It is a tragic thing to cry alone because this means we have built walls around our lives, walls so high that nobody else can see over them. Our tears not only express the deep wells of our feelings but they also make us one with all men who have ever loved or tried to reach out in a tender and caring way to anybody else. Our tears, Dickens said, are "rain upon the blinding dust of earth, overlying our hard hearts." Our tears redeem us when they reveal us clearly to another, unshielded from the consequences or risks that are involved in being human.

If we have cried ourselves, we find something of ourselves to give back to the suffering and sorrowful all around us. We need not move away from them, bidding them to hide their tears because they hurt us so much. We have gone along the same human path and we understand how, in our grief, the presence of another person can bring a certain wholeness to our sorrow. We give life when we learn from our own weeping how to give ourselves with gentleness and compassion to the sighs and struggles of other people. The psalmist was no stranger to weeping and neither was the Lord who cried over Jerusalem and at the death of his friend Lazarus. St. Paul tells us that the whole earth groans and cries out, longing for fulfillment. Mature tears are signs of the same kind of longing, a kinship with a world as yet unfulfilled. Our tears tell us that we are alive, that we have roots in the lives of others, and that we have been touched by the warmest of suns, human love. We should resolve that nobody we love ever has to cry alone.

LOVE'S DICTIONARY: THINGS IT ISN'T

AS many ways as the wind blows, in that many ways and more, men describe love. A man might easily get confused by the many definitions that can be heard these days. This is a special problem for the young who are just starting life and who want, more than anything else, to understand love. The Christian knows that the test of what anybody says about love is always the Gospels, not as a historical book from which all the vitality has been drained by too much expert exegesis, but as the living words that open us to a loving way of life. Indeed, some of the driest and least appealing definitions of love have come from various preachers who have studied the Gospels more than they have lived them. Love that does not have a human face is not love at all.

So we have had a lot of people around who have given love a bad name. They do not deliberately distort it; it is more a case of their never having known or experienced a love that really held together in their lives. There is no cry sadder than that of a person who does not know the meaning of love. For this person, love has always been a mercurial substance, slipping away each time they reach for it. Many search for love all their lives and the lucky ones are healed by it when they finally find it. But many others keep on searching, with a growing and grim knowledge of broken promises, hearts and relationships, never quite getting hold of the love that they desperately want to believe is still out there waiting somewhere for them.

Is love, then, something people learn about only the hard way? That would not be entirely true, although there is no love that does not have its full share of suffering. It is just that it is cruel to mislead people who want and need love with formulas that simply cannot deliver what they promise. There is suffering and struggle enough in the best of love without permitting the pain that does not have to be there. But people are desperate for love, and they will, in defiance of their own wisdom and experience, try almost anything to get it. They will, as we know, take advice on love from perfect strangers when they would hardly ever do the same thing with their money. So the astrologers, the soothsayers and other assorted prophets of hopeful romance survive and grow rich on mankind's hope for a touch of love in life.

It is a betrayal of trust to deceive the young (or to agree to their own self-deception) into thinking that they already understand love just because they long for it so. All too often we give them neither the example nor the sense of realism that genuine love demands. There are many voices telling us all, young and old, about love, and it is important to reflect on both what it is and what it isn't.

For example, love is not soft, although it is gentle. There is a big difference. Softness is an undeveloped quality, something that gives way easily because it has no structure to hold it together. Gentleness is that wonderful grace-note of strength, something that expresses a person's qualities and character when these have been burnished free of hurting blemishes. Love is not the powerlessness of a personality too weak to hurt another; it is rather the tenderness of strength that is under control.

Love cannot be totally passive, although some of its definitions are streaked through with this quality in the age of Aquarius. This passivity is indicative of a shying away from the sharp edges of life and reflects a tendency to look away from, rather than at, the world as it really is. Anything can look beautiful if you stay far enough away from it; and it looks even better when our vision has been modified with drugs and alcohol. This passivity which rejects life is at the root of the spurious softness that so many celebrate as love. This passivity is a cop-out on life if ever there was one. It dodges away from the responsibility for another person that is part of love. Passivity shrinks back and, in effect, says to life: Respond to me and make me feel loved. But life, in one of the laws of love, says that love does not come to those who are unwilling to love.

This passivity has other characteristics that are worth noting. There is an air of coolness about it, a detachment that is prized by the people who don't want life to hurt them. Involvement with another person demands something more than the good feelings for which the passive settle. But the code of coolness says that good feelings, the pleasure of another's company, or "having sex together" is possible without really giving of oneself. You can hold back and protect your emotions and save yourself from hurt through the strategy of non-involvement. So people make no claims on each other, pretending that their interaction leaves no permanent traces in life, and that they can move back from each other with no harm done. No real investment of the self; no need then to pay the high interest rate of emotional hurt either.

This kind of coolness may keep people at a seemingly safe distance from one another but it will never lead them to an understanding of love. In fact, this path leads to the emotional desert of loneliness where there are no refreshing oases because there are no people. There is a long and aching loneliness ahead for the cool and the passive who think they are cutting it when they are really only cutting themselves off from life.

There is an old saying that we can dislike the sin but we must always love the sinner. So too, we may dislike the counterfeit love that is common these days, but we must still love the counterfeit lovers. If any of us have been blessed enough to know real love in our lives, then we have to share it with the people who have lost their way in their search for its meaning. The Gospels tell us that we can never keep our love just for ourselves, that the sign of the Spirit's presence is love that is given away as freely as it is received. Our task, then, is not to condemn the misguided or the insensitive but to share our vision and experience of love with them.

HAPPINESS SEEMS SIMPLE ENOUGH . . .

. . . NOT too much to ask of life surely, not an excessive blessing to pray for, nor a grace beyond the powers above to give. And yet it seems to be granted only intermittently at best, and in small doses at that. We spend more time seeking it and more energy stalking it than we do on almost anything else. There seems to be something wrong here, when so many people have so much difficulty achieving and holding on to the very thing they want most.

I have written before about happiness and its inner nature, which is harder for man to unlock than that of the atom. It is more a by-product of doing something worthwhile than a commodity that can be directly sought. And its heightened moments have only a half-life; they pass quickly but they leave a deep and healing kind of peace behind in our hearts. "Happiness," as poet Robert Frost once wrote, "makes up in height for what it lacks in length."

But what, you ask, is the kind of worthy goal from which happiness is a spin-off? Probably the surest path to happiness, but one that is as narrow as the biblical way into heaven for a rich man, is through getting close to other persons. So often, however, that seems like turning one's back on happiness and opening a door to everybody's grief; it can mean a messy kind of involvement, an entangling kind of enterprise that throws chains around the heart which always hurt and sometimes break it. And, because of these seeming terrors, men walk cautiously, sizing each other up like wary boxers before they get too close. The way to stay content, they feel, or at least to stay safe, is to stay at a distance from others.

It is this kind of attitude towards others that generates alienation and loneliness, the twin specters that make man's heart cold even while he is trying to buy or seduce a little happiness in all the ways the world has told him it could be found. But his ambition turns out to be a petty tyrant giving him no rest and no happiness either.

No, the happy man is the one who works at being close to others in a respectful and loving way. He doesn't get close by taking, but only by giving to others, and learning then how to receive from them in turn. A happy man knows that intimacy is not easy and that fidelity demands that he give himself along with his word on a continuing basis. Being close to others demands that we keep on learning, both about ourselves and those we love. Most of all, I guess, it means that we prize others not as possessions but as persons who need our freeing love to keep going in the way that is right for them in life. That is the kind of love we read about in the Gospels, the love that the Spirit gives us when we are brave enough, even when we don't think we are strong enough, to stick with others through the hazards of life.

BAD WEEKS

WE have known about bad days for some time. They come up in the calendar regularly, more often than not without giving any warning. They are trap doors through which we fall end over end during the daylight hours when nothing seems to go right. They are no fun but they are a lark compared with the black humorless phenomenon that arrived this fall, the curse of the bad week. After all, a bad day is only a tough twenty-four hours, but a whole week makes life into a minefield from which there seems to be no escape. One could almost believe in the existence of meddlesome gods beyond the clouds who have had this giant economy size misery on the drawing boards for some time, just waiting for the right moment, which for us is the wrong moment, to put it on the market. The bad week has arrived and, except for the Excedrin people, nobody but the grinning gods are happy about it.

To string together seven bad days is almost as hard as assembling a block of Fifth Avenue real estate. By the law of averages something good is almost bound to happen in the midst of even the worst days; a good meal, a ray of unexpected sunshine, a smile from a passing stranger, a daydream of pleasant release. The new bad week allows for none of these. Things go wrong and they keep going wrong all through the seven day period. Even Friday, as in "Thank God, It's Friday!" doesn't help. The bad week is not your common up and down brace of days; it is all bad, unrelieved and unalloyed. People have been sending in reports of bad weeks from all over the country.

You can tell that the new bad week has arrived because you do not have to ask people about it. They tell you right off, almost without thinking about it. "That was a bad week!" they will say, too worn out even to ask for a consoling drink, just intent on reporting that it has gone and that they have somehow survived. Bad weeks have been a boon of sorts for those men who wear signboards that read "Repent," but they are hell on people making investments, big decisions, or leaving on vacations. Sometimes bad weeks are confused with the signs of the times. It was in a bad week recently, for example, that Dr. Billy Graham announced that he perceived the indications that the end of the world was at hand. It was also the week of the pornography report, the campus unrest report, the death of Nasser, and the beginning of the end for the big red baseball machine from Cincinnati. And you, what happened to you that week? Chances are that you would just as soon not talk about it.

The bad week is obviously a serious social problem, at least as bad as pollution, and dizzying in its prospects for misleading and discouraging mankind. There does not seem to be much else we can do but warn people about it until the President appoints a commission to look into it. But you know what kind of weeks lie in wait for presidential commissions. The very fact that we know about the phenomenon is, however, a great help in itself. This knowledge will keep you from thinking that you are falling apart, selling your stocks short, or buying unseen land in Arizona. It might give you the courage to hold on because you recognize the face of the enemy and as a result you won't feel so isolated about it. Maybe a Christian view will help us to be patient with our bad weeks and prevent us from spreading the infection to the cheerful and innocent bystanders around us. In any case do not be too alarmed when your next malaise clings to you like big city smog. The bad week has arrived and will be around for some time yet.

WHAT'S WRONG WITH SAYING, "I DON'T KNOW"?

THERE is a little of the con man in the best of us and it comes out especially at those times when we don't know what we are talking about. Most of us, of course, want to appear knowledgeable and, to some degree at least, sophisticated. Ah, to be a man on the in; that little urge is capitalized on by the thousands of merchandisers who want to sell us some of the various trappings of wisdom. And it is this same little urge that leads us to exaggerate, fabricate and generally misinform the world around us.

How many of us there are who automatically use certain phrases that seem to cover our ignorance and make us appear well-informed and in control of our particular piece of twentieth century turf. For example, during the current stock market slide men who have trouble balancing their checkbooks have called upon the phrase "technical correction" to explain the situation. The wonder of phrases like this is that they make you sound intelligent and they discourage your hearer from asking further questions because he does not know what a technical correction is either. It's the same kind of thing that leads a man to diagnose any and every automobile problem with the words, "It's probably the points." This phrase has a gritty, manly quality to it, and could seemingly be used only by persons who have travelled to the far reaches of the masculine game preserve and come back with the trophy of manhood. Then there is the medical phrase that makes you actually feel you are wearing a white coat with a stethoscope shoved into the side pocket, that phrase that we can apply to everything: "There's a lot of that going around this year." Some time ago comedians Bob and Ray gave their annual medical award to the doctor who first uttered these now famous and useful words. In fact, the words do seem to have a semi-curative or calming effect on the sick over whom they are uttered.

You don't need a stock phrase, of course, to let the con man out of you. Sometimes all you need do is nod your head and grunt in varying tones of agreement or disagreement. There are times, also, when we go way beyond this and, through more active storytelling techniques, let people think that we have knowledge that we do not really possess. But occasionally that gets us in pretty deep and we have a very difficult time extracting ourselves while at the same time preserving some measure of face or dignity. In the long run, the momentary delicious feeling of being on the inside and being competent gives way to uneasiness at keeping the threads of all our claims pulled together.

It is an amazing thing, this minor temptation to make it appear that we know what we really do not know, and every one of us is subject to it. There is, however, something refreshing about the man who can say, "I don't know," when that is actually the case. What comes through in a person like this is his genuineness, and this can make up for a lot of other shortcomings. Only a person with very deep needs to impress others has to say something on every subject, and he does this because he is never done proving himself. Research on human relationships has shown that few things are more destructive than pretense. In the same way, nothing is more helpful than the simple truth, even when it consists in an admission of ignorance. In friendship, psychotherapy or marriage, the truth is much better than the urge to con the other person into thinking we know something when we do not.

The truth can hurt, and people can unwisely use it at times for just such a purpose. I am not talking about that as much as the more familiar and less hostile tendency to think that the truth will not be good enough and that we must substitute something else in its place. People who do this habitually are afraid that others will consider their real selves inadequate and will reject them because of it. As a matter of fact, others despise their phoniness much more than their ignorance. We get by only with what is real about us. Friendship and love develop out of what is genuine about us in relationship to others. Con men end up conning themselves into terrible loneliness. So watch out, because there's a lot of that going around.

DISCOURAGEMENT

WE have talked about a lot of common human experiences but there is none that men know better than that of discouragement. It dries up a man's soul and seems to dig a crevice in his heart; it withers a spring garden like the biblical fig tree; the future which may have looked bright just a few hours before is suddenly spoiled with the black clouds of despair.

Discouragement can arrive like that, unannounced, unexpected and quite unprepared for. A man feels all the air drained out of him when discouragement overwhelms him without warning. But discouragement can also be a slow draining away of our energies, with the fibers holding the self together giving way only gradually. In either case the discouraged person finds that it is hard to go on. In fact, so wearisome does life seem that he sometimes is not sure that he wants to get his strength back at all. It is just too painful to return to the daily round with which he is so familiar— hard to get up in the morning, hard to smile and hard to nudge oneself through the day. Discouragement makes a man want to give up and say, "To hell with it," about a whole variety of things in his life: trying to do the right thing for himself and others; keeping at his job or keeping his promises; caring even for those he loves with all his heart.

The person in the grip of discouragement does not respond to the smiling reassurances that shatter like glass as soon as they are uttered. He just crawls down more defensively into his depression when somebody sings out, "Things aren't as bad as you think," or, "Don't feel so bad. Things are bound to get better." In his heart he knows these well-wishers are wrong, not because things won't get better but because of the false tone in their voices. The discouraged man just feels more estranged when people offer him bluff heartiness as an antidote for the infection of every day discouragement.

Everybody knows that discouragement has a way of wearing off and we are sometimes hard pressed to explain why it does so.

When it is heavy upon us, however, we need the presence of somebody other than the incurable optimist. We need someone who can truly be with us during the worst moments of our depressed feelings, someone who can touch us humanly and be a source of hope for us. Some of the more tragic scenes in life are acted out in the lives of the lonely and discouraged people who have no one to share with them their empty and painful moments.

The person who can make himself truly present to someone in the midst of discouragement brings something deeper than easy reassurances. He brings the qualities that say, "I've been through this myself and I know how you feel. It is because of this that I can be with you in this discouragement and stay with you through it." People who can do this make a difference in the lives of others. They bestow courage where it is lacking and breathe hope into others who are plagued with visions of despair. They literally encourage others because they can put into them something of themselves. This kind of encouragement through entering into another's melancholy does not take great training and it doesn't take very much time. Instead it takes sensitivity to the human struggle, strength that comes from some sureness about our own identity, and a readiness to give ourselves rather than just good wishes to others.

There are people who feel too old or too shy to march in picket lines these days but who still want to make some contribution of service to the lives of others. They feel too self-conscious to be where the action is but they are ready to do something for their neighbor in a less dramatic and less publicized way. For these people (and for everybody else, of course) the opportunities to be sensitive to the discouragements of our fellow men are everywhere. These may be found in our own families, in the lives of our friends, or among the lonely exiles in hospitals and nursing homes all around us. In an age when people are growing weary of those who feel that relevance comes from tearing something down, being a source of encouragement to others is about as positive a thing as a person can do. It is a way to love, a way of making the Spirit present, and a way of giving life to those who need it more than anything else.

IS IT REALLY THE SPIRIT SPEAKING?

WE are often told that to lead a good Christian life we must listen to the Spirit and give ourselves over to what he asks. This advice, however, inevitably prompts the question: How can I tell if it is really the Spirit who speaks to me? A now worn out rule of thumb based on Christian asceticism formerly guided our behavior. If something hurt enough or went counter to our own inclinations, then it was almost surely the work of the Spirit in us. If the task were dry and unappealing it clearly seemed the kind of thing we ought to do. But man has been redeemed from this self-punishing kind of puritanism which gave him such a narrow gauge for measuring his Christian response. He knows full well that the Spirit asks first of all that a man give his wholehearted best far more often than a grudging acceptance of the worst in life. The Spirit asks us, for example, to do many of the things we really want to do, such as ending our loneliness, fulfilling ourselves, and finding relationships of trustworthy love with others. These challenges match our deepest desires; and they are at the same time extremely demanding. The Spirit does not close man off from the goal of a full life; it makes him realize how much of himself he must give if he is to attain the most profound aspirations of his being.

While man wonders about the voices within himself, he is not helped much in hearing the Spirit by some of the voices that are outside of himself. There are many who do not trust much in the Spirit and who do not trust much in man's ability to respond to the Spirit on his own. These people have a passion for control, as if they could harness the energy of the Spirit to their own judgment and tell man how and when and to what degree he should respond. These people are very uneasy about freedom as a condition for life in the Spirit; they are afraid of freedom and troubled by the problems experienced by growing Christians. They are full of warnings and cautions as though the Spirit could speak only through the motivation resulting from a fear of doing something wrong. These are poor interpreters for the Spirit in a world grown weary of a religion which offers a way of life that is marked only with danger signs.

The Christian is called to something greater than cautionary steps in the name of the Gospel. He is called, as we read in Mark's Gospel, "to speak an entirely new language," one which retires the vocabulary of fear and invites man to a fuller share of life under the Spirit. This "new language" is not a miracle of being able to speak in a tongue that one has never learned. It is rather the wonder of being able to love in a way that can be learned only through commitment to the Spirit. This power changes the face of the earth because it changes the hearts of men.

If a man wonders whether it is the Spirit speaking within himself he can always measure what he hears against the Gospels. There is a wholeness in the life of a person who lives by the Spirit, an integrity that is not destroyed by the stresses of the life in which he finds himself. A man of faith fits together and his actions flow from a consistent pattern of Gospel convictions. He does not turn restlessly from one cause to another, groping for direction rather than giving a testimony of faith. He brings this sense of wholeness to all the events of his life because his reactions have their source in the Spirit that lives deep within him.

The person touched by the Spirit does not seek emotional experiences for his own sake. This, unfortunately, is sometimes the case in the lives of the contemporary hysterics who glory in the subjective experience of what they choose to call the working of the Spirit. Often enough, however, these are merely examples of a new sentimentality, a relatively undeveloped search for a religious feeling that goes no further than the individual himself. The Gospel is still the test, and the service of others is still the sign of those who are truly living in relationship to the Spirit.

The Spirit leads us to growth and sharing and away from selfishness and the manipulation of other people. The person who lives by the Spirit is not very self-conscious about it but he can be recognized readily because of the incarnational cycle of his life with others. He comes to life in relationship to others; he is willing to die to what keeps him from loving them better; and he gives new life to them even as he discovers a richer life for himself in the process. If we want to know whether we are being guided by the Spirit, we can ask whether we are being led into truly redemptive relationships with others. If we are not, then it is some voice other than the Spirit's to which we are attending.

Another sign is the seal of peace on the lives of those who truly respond to the Spirit. These people know that life is serious but they are not grim; they know that life is a struggle but they do not mistake it for a battle; they are able to face death but they are filled with life. Peace is the gift guaranteed to those who are willing to live by the Spirit, a peace that is not a truce with life but something that is deep and serene. This peace is not produced by tranquilizers but by truly facing life with a deep commitment to following the Spirit. It is a peace that cannot be pretended but that can almost be touched, a peace that fills and transforms the world all around us.

HOW NOT TO BE HELPFUL

LIFE runs, if it runs at all, on the energy we generate through believing in and loving each other. When the world runs out of that
it will have no power supply left at all, no matter how many new
caverns of oil are discovered under the tundra. When man's supply of trust is exhausted, the world will be chilled for good and the
night that falls will last forever. We have a terrible power to
plunge our fellowman into darkness by suspending or holding
back our belief in him. Unfortunately, we sometimes do that just
at the wrong moment, just at the moment, in fact, when someone
is in great need of the support that comes from our confidence in
him. Of all the ways there are not to be helpful, suspension of trust
is close to the head of the list.

We say, however, that it is hard to keep hoping in other people,
even in those who are closest to us in our family or circle of
friends. We hedge on hope and trust because we accumulate so
many scars in giving it out to other people who then blow the
whole thing and disappoint us bitterly. So we get over the idea of
being cheerfully optimistic about our children or our friends and
their good intentions and brave promises. We have seen, we say,
too many compromises made in the course of life to believe un-
qualifiedly in other people. We hold back, muttering to ourselves
"Well . . . ," "Maybe . . . ," "You'll never make it," or something else
that tells the truth about our feelings toward the other. And that
feeling, that strong current rolling across our psyche, is what we
communicate to others, no matter what we say in words to them.

If there is one thing that takes the wind out of a man, it is the
sudden and uneasy realization that his friend or his brother does
not really trust him, that he is on the outside after all, that he is
looked on as someone who might do the wrong thing rather than
someone trying to do the right thing. That is a crushing blow
especially for a growing person who so much needs an older person to believe in him and let him work out some decision or solve
some problem in his own way. For a grownup it can be a discour-

aging experience to discover that friends he relied on are a little skeptical about his trustworthiness after all. Take the edge off your belief in somebody and you may do just the thing that guarantees he will make a mess of something. When a man feels that others do not trust him fully, he finds it hard to keep on trusting himself.

There is no doubt that we can be foolish in giving support to other people when we do not know much about what they are doing, or when we are not close enough to them to be real about it. There are all kinds of reasons for staying at a distance, or for warning people about their possible mistakes. That is easy to do because it doesn't cost anything and it is the most cautious hand to play in human relations. We won't make many mistakes if we follow that course; we won't have many friends either. Instead, our lives will be filled with people we are afraid of or afraid for. This may be a defensively secure way to live but it is also an unhappy way.

The Christian must move from feeling responsible *for* other people to feeling responsible *to* other people. There is a big difference, as wise men and real lovers can tell you. But sticking with other people even as we grant them the freedom to make what they will of their own decisions and their own lives is a hard lesson to learn. Not even husbands and wives are responsible *for* each other; their love stays alive when they are able to be responsible *to* each other and that takes large stringless investments of belief.

Never have men been so tempted to give up on each other as they are in our day, to say "To hell with it," to save themselves and to salvage what they can of the possible happiness in their own lives. And so never have men needed more the generous kind of support that makes the Christian's commitment to other people the most creative and confronting development in the history of the world. The world needs us to believe and to trust, not as cynical schoolmasters ready to punish the failures we can already foresee, but as persons who live by and give life through the Spirit. And it might be a good idea to begin with each other today —or at least to resolve not to give up on each other today.

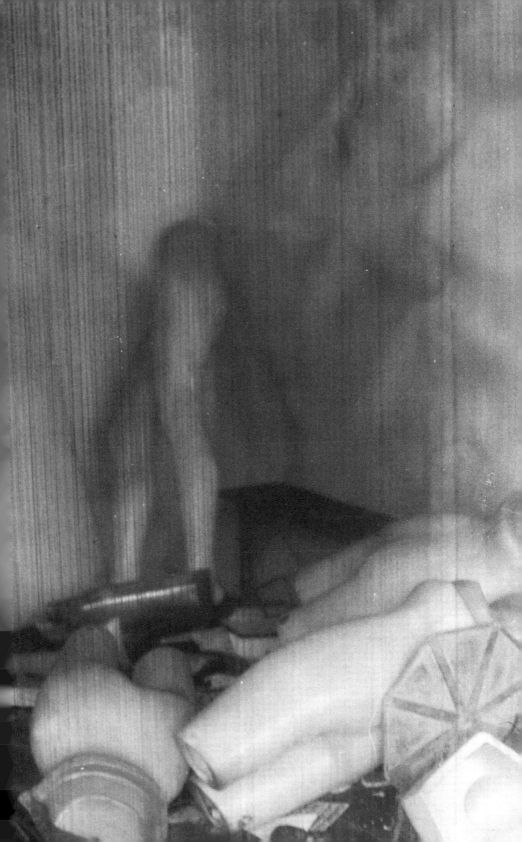

THE MAN WHO PUT
THE WORLD AT A DISTANCE

JAMES B. spoke with me recently and it was not easy for him. He said that he had suddenly discovered, in his mid-forties, that he had no friends, that nobody seemed to like him, and that his heart felt clammy from a loneliness he neither wanted nor understood. Here he was at a time when he theoretically should have been enjoying what he has achieved in life and yet he felt empty, unsatisfied, and inconsolably alone. James B. is not an unusual person; there are many people like him and most of them have no idea what to do about themselves. They dread the years of life that lie before them.

Actually, James B. made his life exactly the way it is; he is not a victim, he is the fashioner of his own situation but he does not understand it at all. He is an extremely intelligent person with advanced degrees, who, until very recently, found himself always absorbed, somewhat like Ebenezer Scrooge, with the business at hand. I have seen a dozen different James B.'s in various roles, from parish priest to college professor to corporation executive and county judge. They are all the same. They substitute the use of their great intelligence for a more balanced development of themselves. In their twenties and thirties they get away with it more easily. They are, after all, on the way up in their various endeavors in life and they handle the emotional side of their existence by creating distance between themselves and other people, a cool, intellectual distance, a brook too broad for leaping. It is a functional distance; it saves them from the price of personal involvement when they have no time for it or little feeling of need for it. They keep everyone at a distance and pursue their own goals undistractedly. And many of them are very successful. It is just that sooner or later, this kind of life catches up with a man, especially when he looks around in midlife and wonders what it all means.

James B. is a perfect example of the type. Brilliant and frequently right on matters at issue, B. *had* to be right all the time.

He measured his relationships by the amount of argumentation he needed to employ in order to prevail. And argumentation became a style with him. No discussion was free of it, no matter how trivial, because he used it to reassure himself of his own excellence and to keep people at a safe distance at the same time. Relationship through constant dissent was his style—a closed mind making what he thought was a secure passage through life.

But now he has the job he wanted and the degree he worked so hard for and the presumed esteem of it all. He even has some kind of respect from other people who always knew him as a kind of argumentative fellow. But he doesn't have any love to speak of, and the people who could have been his friends got tired of arguing with him long ago. Now he is lonely and afraid and life looks like a long antiseptic corridor. Even he is tired of fighting with people. It is quite late for James B. to begin restructuring his life but it isn't too late. He can put himself back into the world of men. It will not, however, be easy. The distance he must travel is exactly as far as he moved away from men on his own years ago.

"DO NOT GO GENTLE . . .

. . . INTO that good night." So wrote Dylan Thomas, the Welsh poet. Rage, he said, rage against the dying of the light. The trouble is that we live in an age in which people have increasingly justified going quite gently and quite passively into more than the good night of death. We have gone a long way in rationalizing our way out of ever having to face and work through pain, anxiety, or even an occasional sleepless night. Better by far to take the appropriate pill that puts pain and bad moods behind us, the prescription that lets us lie down in limbo for a while. No raging here; just a search for quiet and for at least a few moments when life doesn't hurt quite so much. Well, who is to blame modern man, harried and criticized on every side, from taking whatever relief he can find?

The next time you reach for that tranquilizer or that drink ask yourself whether it might not be good to meet the pain or loneliness head on for a change. This is not an invitation to masochism or a tireless condemnation of drugs. Perhaps pain can only be conquered by taking it on as any enemy who must be faced down with quarter neither given nor requested. Man has more resources than he usually thinks; he may never discover them, and therefore never discover himself fully, if he does not enter the pain and suffering that test his depths and test them true. There is a place in life for the experience of pain, not for its own sake, but because it burns the dross off a man in a way that nothing else can.

If a man never fights the battle of suffering out in the open, with full consciousness of what it is all about, he may miss something that is essential to being fully grown. He will miss the full measure of friendship which takes on its meaning, not in the passed cups of celebration, but in the moments when anguish is shared; he will never know real love because in trying to perpetuate romance he will not face the fierce and lonely moments when lovers look like strangers to each other; he will not know the full face of life because he has been afraid to look steadily into the eyes of death.

Man estranged from pain will hardly be the figure we have known all through history. He will be like a child overmedicated against the infant diseases so that he never builds up a strong inner immunity against them; the man who never learns to live with pain only makes himself more vulnerable to it. I am not defending the large measure of unnecessary suffering that is found everywhere in life. No one in his right mind would do anything but attempt to lessen this in all its forms. I refer to the inevitable sufferings of life, the pains that shape our existence, the pains that must be faced because they cannot be fended off. Man who names the birds and the beasts must put the right name on his agonies if he is to do battle with them and down them.

"We are healed of a suffering," Marcel Proust wrote, "only by experiencing it to the full." Redemption lies, then, in sifting our real from our fancied problems and in dealing with both of them realistically. Some people cover their real problems with imaginary problems to such an extent that they never can tell the symptom from the real suffering. They have terrible headaches in place of working through the difficulties of a tangled personal relationship; in fact the headaches excuse them from even understanding where the real problem lies. That kind of person misses the self-identity that emerges when we truthfully confront the real challenges of living. He cannot experience his suffering to the full because he won't let himself see what it is. And so he cannot find or offer redemption through the experience. People are ordinarily afraid that they will miss the meaning of life if they miss one of its possible pleasures; they run a far greater risk of missing its meaning when they shy away from its sufferings.

The Christian is familiar with all of this. He knows that Christ dreaded but actively accepted the pain that was inseparable from his role as the redeeming servant of mankind. Christ knew what men would do to him and neither looked away from the suffering itself nor from understanding the complex motives of his persecutors. He faced and conquered suffering and death; he did not surrender to them. Our involvement in the continuing mystery of redemption bids us to deal with our own personal pains in a similar fashion. This is not the stoic refusal to admit that pain can lay a hand on you. It is rather the Christian's active entrance into his sufferings, his standing up against them or grappling toe to toe with them while the light lasts; that is the way of life because that is the way of resurrection.

The Spirit comes to the Christian who remembers the worth of fighting the good fight and of not wasting his blows on the empty air. St. Paul spoke of keeping faith that way. Perhaps he meant that his refusal to go gently into the night of suffering was a way of keeping faith with himself and his true identity as a man and as an apostle. So rage a little against the real suffering in your life; it may well be the price of your soul.

THERE'S A LITTLE BOY IN
THE BIGGEST MAN . . .

. . . AND he is forever trying to get out. You can see him clearly
if you look close enough. There is, as you know, the wonderful and
winning innocence of the man who has kept the best of his boy-
hood alive into his adult years. He still looks with wonder at the
world; his eyes are bright and inquisitive, and when you ask him
a question, it is the truth that comes out because he has never
mastered the deceitful arts. There is something marvelous in the
man whose fundamental goodness has never been corrupted by
all the badness he has had to look at in life. His playful energy and
his transparent openness are incorporated into his grown-up style;
his presence disarms us because he neither attacks us nor raises
defenses before us. That's the little boy who still likes locomotives,
ball games, and surprises, the little boy in the big man whose out-
line can still be made out by wives and mothers, the little boy who
is earnest and good and who never wants to hurt anybody.

But there is another little boy in a lot of us who is quite different
from this, the one who is part puppy dog tails, and he is the one
we must keep an eye on. This is the obstinate little boy who long
ago put his head down against growing up, preferring to hold on
to his childhood strategies in order to try to get his way with the
world around him. "A boy's will is the wind's will," Longfellow
wrote. For these boys, however, it blows in only one direction, the
way that will enable them to get something out of it. This man
may look grown-up but the spoiled little boy inside him keeps
stamping his foot and insisting on his own childish way all the
time. This man may get married, but the odds are that he will get
another mother rather than a wife. And he loves the care and
feeding she may lavish on him (particularly if she is the kind of
woman who is looking for a child more than for a husband), never
able to get enough of it.

The little boy inside this man is not the wide-eyed and loving
child described before; he is rather a self-centered and hostile lit-

tle fellow who cannot get himself out of the foreground in any view he takes of the world. He has got it straight about loving himself first; there is no doubt about his priorities in that regard. It's just that he has it all mixed up, and it is self-infatuation and self-absorption more than any kind of healthy self-respect that marks his attitude toward himself. And so there is little room for anybody else in this man's affections; he is like the strange races of sinister children who coldly inhabit science fiction these days and who work untold harm before the antibodies arrive to neutralize them.

This boy-man reveals himself, however, in the way in which he handles crises in his life. That is when his real style is clear for everyone to see. The psychologists speak of regressive behavior as an option for some people when they are under pressure, and so it is in this case. He uses as an adult the tricks he used as a child to cover up his mistakes or to get out of some responsibility or other. For example, to avoid conflict he may use the old childhood device of sudden illness just the way he did when he wanted to miss an exam in school. That way he gets to stay home in a nice warm bed while his wife mothers him and the cold winds of the world blow by. When such behavior is actually a replay of just what the individual did do when he was a child, it is called retrogression, a literal going back to an earlier time. There is another kind of regressive behavior which is termed primitivation. We see it in the person who makes a crying scene when the heat is turned on him so that everybody feels bad and has to comfort him. Another classic example is the person who gets into a fight as his way of settling disputes; no reasoning, calm, or patience for him, just wade right in there and settle things with your fists. That is not an adult thing to do, no matter what name we use to describe this behavior.

As for little boys in grown-up men, we need more of the first kind and fewer of the latter. Perhaps we can listen and hear which boy is inside us and we will be wiser and more grown up if we learn a lesson from this. And, as for dealing with others, it is good to be able to tell the difference between the good boy who has become a man and the spoiled boy who has never gotten anywhere. I think the children Christ let come to him were of the first variety, and it may just be that the little child who "will lead them" is not literally a little child at all, but a grownup who has never lost the best aspects of being young and innocent.

LEARNING TO LOVE

THERE may not be many experiences more damaging to a man's psyche than to find the love he thought was real going to pieces in his very hands. Perhaps we can be more helpful to others if we realize that these shocks come mostly to people who are just learning how to love. This experience, which is common in both friendship and love, is most prevalent during the growing years we used to call adolescence—whenever these may come in a person's life. It is a hazard of growing, a danger to anyone opening up for the first time to the magic of getting close to someone else. In fact, the experience sometimes must take place in friendship before it can take place in love. It is hard, in other words, to move out of oneself and toward other people into the great adventures of friendship and love. This is an important period of life, this time when an individual first senses the mysterious blend of idealism and deepened self-consciousness that allows him to perceive other people in a new way. The German author Thomas Mann catches an aspect of this experience in his famous story *Tonio Kroger*. It opens with Tonio waiting after school for his friend Hans; they had agreed to go for a walk together. Tonio is deeply wounded when he notices that Hans had almost forgotten their engagement. He forgives Hans, however, when he sees his friend's remorse. But they still feel this near-misunderstanding as they start their walk:

> . . . Tonio did not speak. He suffered. His rather oblique brows were drawn together in a frown, his lips were rounded to a whistle, he gazed into space with his head on one side. Posture and manner were habitual.

> Suddenly Hans shoved his arm into Tonio's, with a sideways look—he knew very well what the trouble was. And Tonio, though he was silent for the next few steps, felt his heart soften.

> "I hadn't forgotten, you see, Tonio," Hans said, gazing at the pavement, "I only thought it wouldn't come off today because it was so wet and windy. But I don't mind that at all, and it's jolly

of you to have waited. I thought you had gone home, and I was cross. . . ."

The truth was, Tonio loved Hans Hansen, and had already suffered much on his account. He who loves the more is the inferior and must suffer; in this hard and simple fact this fourteen-year-old soul had already been instructed by life. . . .

(*Stories of Three Decades*, Alfred A. Knopf, Inc. Copyright 1936)

The same poignant quality edges all the experience of young love and new friendship. A person learns a great deal about himself through these encounters; indeed, he cannot develop without them. But they make him vulnerable to the special hurts and misunderstandings that sweep his heart like an epidemic when he is not sure of his relationship with another. In fact, the person (boy or girl) suffers precisely because there is so much self-concern and self-need involved in this kind of developing love. They do not know it, and they cannot readily admit it, but these relationships are just the beginnings of love—the first wrenching away from their own inner world. And it is not surprising that this learning how to love should be a time for many mistakes. That is what happens when we try to learn anything, and we should not be amazed to see faults, jealousies, and other miscalculations of the heart filling the space known as first love.

Well, why go into all this? Because you cannot help another person unless you have a sympathetic understanding of the elements that go into another's experience. You cannot help suddenly estranged lovers unless you know that this experience is to be expected (rather than unexpected) at this particular time of life when people are beginning to reach out to each other. People will hurt each other—even as they misunderstand each other—in more serious ways than by forgetting about a plan to walk home from school together. Unfortunately, this period of exploration and discovery does not have many guides, despite the fact that we know of the hazardous reefs and landfalls that have always marked its course. In other words, you must let young people learn to love the hard way. Let them travel the painful path of misunderstanding and make mistakes in order that they may learn how hard it is to climb out of their own egos and make room for someone who is truly different from—rather than just an extension of—themselves.

When you understand that first loves are not usually final loves, when you can understand that what is learned is far greater in the long run than what is lost, then you may be able to sit with the young person whose love has just ended and sympathize with a deep and lifegiving compassion. A failure in love does not end it all; the person has, in fact, taken a big step toward a greater capacity for love because his heart has been opened through the experience. What you can do to help is refrain from giving any final answers, and try not to close wounds quickly that must heal slowly from the inside. You must stick with brokenhearted lovers at such moments, not mocking them or falsely encouraging them. If you just make yourself present and convey the understanding that shows that you have had a similar experience in your life, you will help keep a young heart open to love when it comes in a richer, more mature, and more lasting form. You will, in other words, have helped the person learn something new about himself and about life. And to help another learn solidly about the love that still lies ahead is a very great thing indeed.

WHAT DO YOU DO
WHEN NOTHING CAN BE DONE?

THERE is excitement in a demanding and clearly defined challenge; healthy people sometimes exhilarate in solving problems and overcoming obstacles in order to achieve some greater good. Often, the best in man comes out when he can see an attractive goal and can feel the tension of summoning up his inventory of strengths in order to reach it. However, more than the best in man is needed when, despite his desire and willingness to do almost anything, situations arise which render him helpless. What do you do when there is nothing you can do, nothing definite anyway, to make yourself feel that at least you have tried your best or done your damnedest?

Such moments do come into every life—times when there is just no sure guide about what can be done to make things better. A man can feel at a loss then, thrown back on the resources of his spirit, left to rediscover the kind of hope he needs to make his way in the dark. It can happen to parents, for example who have done everything they can for their children; there comes a time when parents must allow their children to make their own decisions about their directions and ideals in life. It can be hard to let go of a young man or woman, especially when he or she seems hardly more than a child. Should one let them go into the unsmiling world when they seem all too vulnerable to the ways in which the world can hurt people? There is, in fact, nothing to do but let them go; you cannot live, grow, or cry for them. But still it is difficult for people to accept this fact; it is hard for them to know when they cannot do anything more than what they have done.

This trying problem comes up in many other situations. It may happen that you have friends—a married couple for example—who are out of touch with each other, their communication shattered, their bitterness against each other sharply honed. Perhaps you want to help. But often there is nothing anyone can do when their wounds are too tender to touch. Occasionally, well-meaning friends display an ironic talent for hurting when they really mean to heal. It is difficult, indeed, to learn the art of being a friend who makes himself available, but who never intrudes. Such a person is the man who has learned what to do when there is nothing to be done.

Or suppose, as can happen so often, the situation is completely out of your hands; there is nothing you could do even if you wanted to. For example, there are heart-rending moments of waiting in hospital corridors and doctors' offices while somebody you love is beyond your words or your touch; they exist for the moment in that hazy atmosphere of unnecessary sickness or uncertain diagnosis where you cannot go yourself no matter how much you ache to do so. There are times when all we can do is wait with those we love, wait for the words we are afraid to hear, or for the decisions we wish did not have to be made. These are the times when we are laid bare as persons, when our interior substance or lack of it becomes plain in the charged space where all distractions fail, when we must face the unknown—with someone we love—as best we can. In these moments we have to tame our restlessness and let our pride die because there is absolutely nothing we can *do*, we can only *be* with the other as fully as we can. And that is as hard as anything in life. It means learning that we do not always have to be doing something in order to love and help another. In fact, it means that we must learn to make ourselves present with another just as we are, putting away our own wishes and fighting off self-pity at the same time. This is precisely the time when our loved ones need *us;* not what we can do or say, but just us, as we are, with them through the long hours when it may take extreme effort to keep our courage from collapsing with the next deep breath. This is the time when we learn to pray again, when we dig deep inside ourselves for the sincerity we might have forgotten. This is the moment of truth—when we learn whether we have guts, or character, or if we have ever learned anything about love. We only appear to be doing nothing. We are really doing the most important thing of all.

THE PROBLEM OF COMMITMENT

I'M sure you have heard the question: Can a person really make a commitment these days? Perhaps you have even asked it yourself. Nowadays we seem to live on a jello-like land, our footing unsure and our hearts unstrung by the never-ending tremors. It is understandably hard to make a hurried passage from a church where everything was solid and secure—where there seemed so many people as well as things you could always count on—to this new territory where there seem to be so few anchor points and moorings. And it is not just the change of rites or styles in the church; it is the change in people that gets you down these days. The ones you relied on yesterday are gone today; priests and religious who used to move serenely toward silver jubilees may now be getting married instead. It makes a person feel the transience of it all; where did that old world of faithful friends, strict rules, but, for all that, good things go? And, in the light of this experience, can anyone make a long-range commitment to anybody or anything anymore?

It is a fair question and it touches married people just as deeply as anybody else. After all, the divorce rate soared in the sixties, and recently one state legislature introduced a bill which would allow three-year, renewable, contract-like marriages. The tenuous nature of marriage vows is graphically underscored by the young who want to avoid all talk of commitment, as though a formal commitment would contaminate a personal relationship because it implies demands from which both parties wish to feel free. Commitment, fidelity, just sticking at it seem to be weighty obligations, burdensome yokes that no one wants to shoulder these days. Has not Alvin Toffler in his book *Future Shock* prophesied *transience* as a characteristic of tomorrow's man? It already seems here for the highly mobile people who, due to their constant moving, have been urged by another social commentator to develop "portable roots." Don't preach to modern man about his not having any lasting city; he knows that all too well.

Well, what about it; can anybody make a permanent commitment anymore? Perhaps we have to remove the question from the theoretical realm, from all the sociological and anthropological observations. Maybe the only way we can answer it is by asking it of ourselves: Can I make a permanent commitment to a certain work or a certain person? Immediately we realize that we need more information—and not just theoretical information—about ourselves before we can frame a response.

What, in fact, do I believe in—truly believe in—as the basis of the way I live? And how much do I know about myself, both my strengths and my weaknesses, so that I have some fair idea of what personal qualities I can commit to others? It is surprising that, until the church and the world seemed to turn suddenly mushy underfoot, many of us never asked ourselves these questions. We presumed more about commitment than we actually knew. Perhaps that was because we relied on others to fashion the answers and to gird up our beliefs for us—people who looked like they knew what they were doing as they prompted us with our lines in life and chalk-marked our entrances and exits. It matters little now, for the time has come when we must ask these questions of and for ourselves. And the more earnestly we ask them, the more we expose ourselves to the cold winds that blow through even the examined life, the more sure we will be of ourselves. For these are the questions that make a person grow.

Fidelity is not, however, just a great weight imposed on us by a blind god behind the clouds; it is not something we learn only to maintain our balance better; it does not, in fact, come under the classification of burden at all. Being faithful, being true to one's self and one's word is intrinsic to our humanity, an essential aspect of confronting ourselves no matter how shifting the sands of life are all around us. I must ask myself whether I take my life, and my continued growth in life, seriously. My fundamental faithfulness must be to my own person, to what is possible and essential for me in order that I might deserve the name of man. The fundamental problem concerns the meaning I want to search out and give to my life; although the questions can be asked by others, the answers can only be given by me.

If I have an inner commitment to my own development, can I imagine that it is something that can be made with reasonable assurance merely for a year or two? Or is it a promise that cannot be quite fully defined in time and space, something too close to the breath of life itself to be contained by any calendar? How, after all, does a person believe in himself, from day to day, or from year to year? Or is it something deeper inside himself, something of the truth about a man that only emerges under the testing pressures of life? And is that truth indivisible so that it cannot be considered, in the long run, as partial or temporary? When you give yourself over to discovering the truth about yourself you must ride this pledge to the very end.

And does not this search for ourselves necessarily lead us toward the truth of others, the others we need in order to find ourselves fully, the others who cannot become truly themselves without us? The voyage of commitment is never made alone; a man cannot, then, be committed only to himself or he will die of the psychological childhood disease of narcissism. He must ask whether he can give himself to another, or to others, not knowing the changes that time, bad luck, and sickness may work on them. I often wonder whether relationships can work at all if they are circumscribed by the conditions that go into temporary loves or friendships. How would it work if, right from the beginning, a man could say, "I'll be your friend until you're in trouble," or "I'll love you as long as I'm not tempted by a younger woman"? Or perhaps, "I'll stay with you while you are healthy and rich." We would laugh at these notions, short-sighted and ill-developed as they are, knowing that you have to give more than this in real love, and be ready to move into darkness, illness, and the loss of beauty, if you care at all about someone else.

We stand on sacred ground when we stand close enough to another to give ourselves without strings, conditions, or codicils written into our commitments. Are such commitments possible? How can one tell unless he has given himself to another, made his heart vulnerable, in order to achieve a sense of life which is deeper than the trembling moment and its dreadful ticking uncertainties. People who work at staying in love, men who keep their words—these are the people alive to God's covenant of help and support as they pursue the truth of their lives and their relationships. Christianity is not glimpsed only in dramatic signs; it is a matter of fact, revealed in multiplied small facts, all of them commitments in faith of one kind or another.

Maybe we cannot put a lasting commitment into words that will endure as long as the commitment. And perhaps it is true that we can learn more about what is expected of us in our own promises to ourselves and to others only as time passes. But permanent commitments are possible, even when theoretically they seem difficult or beyond our reach. That is what keeps us growing, in love and trust, through the power of the Spirit, and helps us to surmount the odds man has always met in becoming himself.

COVETOUSNESS

YOU do not hear the word *covet* very much any more, perhaps because something like coveting has become a way of life and we would rather not think of it in quite that way. For example, the economy would collapse without widespread cultural urges to covet goods of all kinds, useful and unuseful. Covetousness of another's spouse is not uncommon no matter what the color of your collar or the hardness of your hat. The problem is, of course, that a case of the covets merely unleashes desires that are usually not very well understood or integrated in the people who experience them. That is why all their longings and all their acquisitions often leave them unhappy, drowning in the deep red sea of debt. Never have so many people who wanted so many things owed so much money for things they are not happy with after they get them.

And it works the same way for sex. This is a great age for long-distance intimacy and voyeurism for the masses. Entrepreneurs, perspiring freely with erotic enthusiasm, capitalize on the loneliness that lies beneath what we used to call lust by giving mankind a keyhole as big as a movie screen. So we have had an explosion of *Adult* bookstores, even in the small midwestern towns of legendary virtue. These bookstores—more appropriately called *Adolescent* bookstores—provide men a place in which they can fan some warmth out of the fires of their own coveting. However, there is nothing more frustrating than the fantasies, vivid but quickly vanishing, that arouse but never satisfy. That is the trouble with all kinds of coveting; they cause more anxiety and uneasiness than anything else, ravaging rather than giving peace to those who long.

You cannot help but look with compassion on men beset with dreams of things and persons beyond their reach. If we have come to a new yet unnamed emphasis on coveting; we can also see that condemning coveting is not in itself going to help the problem very much. Wisdom bids us to look beneath our longings, to the values that give us a center of gravity and a sense of direction in life. Covetousness—that unruly reaching out for what will never fit or bring happiness to us—is a human wound that heals only from the inside. In other words, "custody of the eyes" does not cut off coveting, and it never has. Enlarging a man's heart, helping him to grow to a deeper vision of life and its meaning, letting him know that the Gospels are good news because they tell us how truly to live—these are the responses that are appropriate for the desolating conflicts that come from too much coveting. Too many of the churches have wasted too much breath trying to control the objects of man's desires on the outside of him, condemning books, films, and bad behavior without helping man to put himself together better on the inside. Covetousness resists the direct attack; it must be transformed by being absorbed in the growth process of the maturing Christian.

Maybe we will begin to deal more effectively with the strangely sown seeds of wanting what we cannot have when we call it by its right name again. In this era when men can speak all the forbidden words out loud, perhaps it is time to speak frankly of the things that cripple us as God's children. Call it covetousness, not bargain-hunting, good economy, or necessary for self-development. This kind of honesty would be particularly helpful as we head into the age of expanded leisure where not all the snowmobiles or ski trips imaginable will make man feel more human or happy. For man needs something better, something he can, with God's help, only get for himself, and only if he begins to deal with values that can never be lost. Those are the gospel values and they bring joy and peace to the man who lives by them.

ISN'T LOVE DANGEROUS?

THAT is the gist of many questions I get both at lectures and through the mail. The question is usually couched in words which reveal longing and uneasiness; it comes out of the hearts of people who want to be part of real life but who also want to do the right thing. Furthermore, the very possibility of love coming into the life of a dedicated person—say a priest or a religious—seems full of danger indeed, especially in view of the news (not exactly headlines anymore but still news) of so many transformations of religious vocations into marriage vocations.

There is, in fact, nothing more powerful and therefore, I suppose, nothing more dangerous than love. And so it has been throughout history. Yet, though there is nothing more dangerous than love, there is nothing so essential to life either. It is one of the dangers we have to face and live with if we seriously intend to live according to the Gospels. We have to face the inevitability of love's entrance into the heart of anyone who opens himself in sincere service to others; a dedicated person makes himself vulnerable to the power of the Spirit whenever he shares himself with others.

Just as dangerous as love, however, is the possibility of a life without love, of an existence which, in the name of virtue, is purged of affection and tenderness, a "proper" kind of life armored against passion or caring. The biggest threat to humanity is a cold life in the sunshine of sharing with others. The real reason that love seems so dangerous is because there is so much fear in the lives of people who defend themselves against the possibility of being close to others. Whenever you are afraid, everything looks dangerous to you.

Yes, love is dangerous; it always has been, and evidently it always will be. But it is also a wonderful enlarging of the self and, in the long run, the only emotion in which we can place our hope. So, live dangerously; it beats not living at all.

I THOUGHT YOU WANTED IT THAT WAY

WITH some such expression lovers often times discover that they have been, with hearts full of the best of good will, defeating the purposes of each other. It is really a relief when they finally find out that, in their separate but misguided efforts to please each other, they have come perilously close to wrecking their relationship. There is relief in this revelation because the people involved may have begun to think that something far more serious was wrong, that they had fallen forever out of phase with each other, and that the magic, as James Thurber used to say, had permanently fled from their marriage or romance. When it finally dawns on them that they are, as dear Mrs. Portnoy used to complain, guilty only of being too good to each other, they know that all is not lost. Perhaps an example will help.

Take the husband and wife who decide—not together, mind you—that each will do whatever they think the other one would really prefer to do during a day they have finally managed to have to themselves. Their resolutions to set aside their private inclinations are noble enough; the man and woman are resolved to sacrifice themselves for the sake of each other, to put aside what each would like to do in order to please the other. The trouble with this kind of resolution, when it is not come to by common agreement, is that it plays on perverse quirks in our nature, even in the moments when we are trying to be most noble. So the husband, who really wants to get the household accounts straightened out, puts these aside because he thinks his wife would like to go shopping and to dinner. The wife, on the other hand and through the same process of private crystal ball gazing, decides to go along with whatever her husband seems to want, even though she prefers to get that spare room cleaned up, a job she has delayed too long. The spare room provides the same emotional valence for the wife as the finances do for the husband; these are the things they both really want to do. But, with the magnificently mistaken notion that the other wants to do something else, they forsake their own wishes. That is where the trouble starts.

There is nothing worse, surely, than self-consciousness martyr-dom—a temptation for each of us when we put aside what we want because we think we know what somebody else wants. When we both make the same mistake at the same time, we enter that strange twilight zone of silent frustration and uncommuni-cated suffering in which we try to please but sense that it is not working. This kind of mistake cuts across all relationships, genera-tion gaps, occupations, and states in life. The trouble arises when we start picking up those little signals that something is inexplica-bly wrong, that for some reason, even though we have made an heroic sacrifice, the day is going downhill, and fast.

We cannot hide those little signs that flare up like measles spots from the fever of offering the wrong thing up for each other. After all, we say, in a shiver of self-pity that actually ruins everything, *we* are making the effort and it just doesn't seem fair that it should be coming to naught. We get a little restless; "Why isn't she enjoy-ing this after the sacrifices I've made?" And she is asking the same thing while trying to keep up a good front: "What's the matter with him anyway? I'm trying to do what he wants."

Now that kind of tension just cannot mount up forever. It al-most seems that the collision course of the day has been charted in the stars. The day itself only collapses, however, in the middle of the afternoon, when one or the other blurts out, "Well, I thought this is the way you wanted it." And the other replies, "You thought this is the way *I* wanted it? And then . . . all hell breaks loose. Of course, by this time it is too late to salvage the day for the purpose of either party. The entire day has been a magnificent failure with nobody enjoying any of it—least of all the final con-frontation about how considerate each party was being of the other.

Well, these things happen, but mostly when we substitute mind reading and being "nice" to each other for our real feelings about things. We sometimes are so afraid to hurt each other's feel-ings in a small way that we end up hurting them in a very large way instead. There is, perhaps, nothing quite so hazardous as meaning well in secret. It just does not work out in reality. You say it can't happen to you? Well, I'd like a report on that a year from now. This is the kind of thing that happens to all of us. It is something that reveals the dangers of the human condition but helps us to recognize each other and forgive each other, not only for our bad intentions, but for our good intentions too. Good intentions, they say, are still what the road to hell is paved with; and people who substitute good intentions for good communication travel that road more than they should. So the next time you get the urge to sacrifice yourself for your loved one, make sure everything is clear right from the start. You can't possibly lose and you might save a lot, including your relationship and, if you're lucky, maybe even the day itself.

FREE AT LAST

THE air nowadays seems filled with sophisticated ladies, streaking across our field of vision on the jet stream of liberation. Some of them seem like brief candles. For example, there is fiery Kate Millett, who, since her bisexual admission, is descending more rapidly than a biblical star. And rising steadily above the horizon now is Germaine Greer, to speak for all the ladies who have freed themselves from the domination of men. Supermale, even super-Mailer, writes in self-doubt in the face of these ladies. Women are free at last but, ungentlemanly as it may seem, the question arises: who is getting free? The answer comes just as clearly: why, men, of course. Don't let Mailer or any of these other ruminative males fool you. Men are winning again, freeing themselves from mature obligations in fundamental and far-reaching ways. In fact, men are freer than ever. With their complaints disguising their pleasure, in the way of men throughout history, they have allowed women to back into a new high-style bondage as the price for some of their isolated victories in the battle for women's liberation.

Little attention has been paid to this fact. Perhaps men like it that way—a little darkness, a lot of anonymity, and a quick drifting away from the point of responsibility that is at the heart of the man-woman relationship. Just as it happens in so much bad fiction, real-life men have slipped into the night leaving their women not so much free as abandoned, not so much liberated as alone in the face of complex problems centering on *her sexual* life. Woman has come, in other words, to have the buck stop with her, neatly placed there by a quickly vanishing and suddenly immune male figure.

It is the woman, after all, who must take the pill; it is the woman, in this new found freedom, who is to decide whether she will have a baby or an abortion; it is the woman who must bear the weight of rebelling against the destiny which she no longer believes to be linked to her biology. Yes, women can decide these things but, while some women boast proudly of their capacity for independent self-determination, it is legitimate to ask whether women should be deciding all these things alone. Is it, in fact, psychologically sensible or even morally permissible to let man escape so easily from such difficult problems? Is man really uninvolved or above and beyond the law? Put briefly, men have never had it so good; they can step away from the exploitation of women; they have taken care of female needs and now they can let women make decisions about the consequences of their behavior with men. Men have not commented on this very much, probably because they know a good thing when they see it. They can continue right into their old age sowing wild oats, rationalizing their behavior with the conviction that woman alone must answer the hard questions about sexual responsibility. The question, then, is not concerned with a woman's right to decide whether or not she will have children—although this is the only thing people seem to talk about these days. Beneath the controversy is the more profound question of what, in the long run, is to become of individuals and of the human race if man is exempted from his responsibility for giving or withholding life in relationship to a woman.

This is to cheat the woman and to make her a captive while seeming to free her. Her liberation becomes an illusion and she is left isolated. No longer the victim of constraining laws or ivy-choked Victorian customs, she is the victim of a view which has far greater long range oppressive possibilities—the willingness of men to employ rationalization as a substitute for wisdom in the conduct of their relationships with women.

This gives man a great out, the escape route of his dreams, a treasure suddenly stumbled upon, the value of which is so staggering that a man dare not breathe a word about it even to his best friend. Unfortunately such sudden wealth unworked for, such marvelous excuses offered gratuitously tend to make a man irresponsible because he never even needs to think about whether he also shares some responsibility for the consequences of sexual experience. Now he can be SUPER-STUD, far freer than woman who must bear the burden of his sexual mistakes and face up to the hard decisions of whether she will bear new life or not.

This is hardly a brave new world; it is, in some ways, more timid and less assertive than the old one. The consequences of allowing man to move off into the unmeasured distance as woman deals with the questions of conception and abortion are numerous. Clearly there will be some effect on family life and on the role of the husband and father as a maker of any decisions at all. This consequence, suspected by few men at the present time, logically proceeds from allowing the woman to bear so much of the burden of whether children will be born or not. So too, one can expect a diminution of the relationship between man and woman, a slow and subtle restructuring, the effects of which may not be noted for many years. Inevitably, if not completely predictably, these effects will be felt.

Perhaps the most important issue centers on the nature of the guiding values which have allowed the present situation to come to pass. It is almost epically remarkable that, despite the tumult and shouting about birth control and abortion, few, if any church-men have stressed the responsibility of the man in all the sacred decisions connected with having children. Perhaps that is because churchmen, being males for the most part, all suffer from the same kind of narrow vision. There are many questions which must be discussed about the role of women in contemporary society and most of them also involve man. Neglecting to discuss the implica-tions of the pseudo-liberation of women perpetuates the male myth and sentences the discussion to suffocate in its own rhetoric while leaving the fundamental question of man's responsibility untouched. The issue is too large for TV talk shows, too far-reach-ing to be left in the hands of highly verbal but otherwise imma-ture discussants. Indeed it is time for all those institutions which understand themselves as committed to the preservation of human values to search out the full dimensions of *human* liberation—both male and female.

WHAT TO DO
WHEN YOU'RE FEELING DOWN

PROBABLY no subject has inspired more advice than that malady, more common than the common cold itself, which has many names and no name at all. I mean, of course, that frayed stage curtain that falls unexpectedly and rudely across our day to leave us without enthusiasm, energy, or even much hope. Call it the blues or the blahs; everybody knows what this experience is like but few of us have learned to cope with it successfully. We usually wait for it to pass, and sooner or later it does; in the meantime we go through the motions of life as best we can. It is like being caught in an airport because of a fog that we can neither pray nor propel away; we just wait in the uncomfortable chairs, a restless and steamy crowd of fellow travelers milling about us, until the overcast lifts away by itself.

But is that all we can do? Not according to those who love to give advice—be it philosophical ("Into each life some rain must fall") or physiological ("Try the Canadian Air Force exercises"). Some of us have tried all of these solutions and ended up wiser, if not less melancholic, for all our exertions. We never feel so good as at the moment when our mood or depression begins to dissipate. "How," we ask ourselves, "did I get over this one?"—thinking if only we could remember this evaporating combination we might apply it earlier the next time we slump into the dumps. But the reasons why we emerge from the blackness are as hard to identify as the reasons we sink into it. What can a man do?

Well, there are several solutions which we can quickly put aside. These include drinking, daydreaming, and drug taking. These are popular ways of escaping from the very real pain of being down. However, their distracting or mollifying effects on us are tragically temporary and when their magic is over we are more depressed than ever—and no closer to understanding why. There is nothing easier to talk oneself into than a couple of quick ones to purge the soul of the day's accumulated dross. Even tranquilizers are socially acceptable in this day and age in which we settle for anything that promises to take the edge off life even for a few hours.

The first step we might take is to remember that ups and downs are rather normal and they do not generally require drastic medicines or overkill responses. There is something to be said for the Far Eastern method of letting ourselves swim with the tide of life even when it is running against us. Thrashing about blindly may cost us more energy and generate more frustration than it is really worth. In other words, most people have cyclic moods and they should not get too upset when they occur. For the average man, a few moments of self-reflection may help him to understand why his emotions have suddenly taken a nose dive. The trouble, of course, is that when we do not feel very well we do not feel like inspecting our emotions either. That is one of the reasons why a little snag in our day can have such a powerfully depressing effect on us. Let me explain.

Suddenly, overcast emotional weather comes from a rapidly forming front of small hurts or disappointments—a big storm touched off by a lot of little lows in our everyday life. For example, upon rising, a man may feel fairly fit and ready to work energetically all day. At breakfast, however, his wife brings up something that takes the air out of him—like telling him that he is beginning to look middle-aged, or that there is some evidence that their oldest son is smoking pot, or that her mother is arriving for a month's visit that very afternoon. In varying ways, these little announcements can depress a man, deflating him and turning what promised to be a good day into a long journey into night. Let us take a closer look at these examples.

The sudden reminder of our mortality is not so startling; we can read the calendar as well as anybody else. It is just that a reminder of that sort usually comes at the wrong moment—it is often out of tune with our general mood and is the kind of information we do not like to think about anyway. This is typical of the small events, so tiny that we are not aware of their impact at the time, which get into our bloodstream with a subtle but sure effect on our general well-being. These are small blows (little murders, if you will) so glancing that we hardly admit them into our consciousness—hardly, in other words, give a name to them when they occur. Their effect is nonetheless telling, in part because the nature of these problems is such that we do not like to say, even to ourselves, that such things bother us. But they are inside us, these psychological viruses of the human condition, and they sap our strength all day long. To handle these situations adequately a man must be willing to trace the path of his depression back to the incident that set it off. This takes time and honesty. It may also require a sense of humor; otherwise we might be appalled at the size or character of the event that laid us low. A good laugh, as we recognize our human frailty, is very therapeutic.

Learning that someone near and dear to you may have a serious problem is a much more obvious source of depression—especially if we get the information at an awkward time when we cannot do anything about it. There is a strange economy in the business of breaking bad news; we frequently do it at the worst possible time for the person to whom we communicate it, e.g., just as the other is going to work, or off on a trip, or after a long day. Half of the depression that follows arises from the frustration we feel because we cannot possibly do anything but worry about the situation at the moment. A man should pause at such a time and think about what he can do and when he can effectively do it. Dealing with the problem realistically, even if it means delaying our response until a better time, will eliminate much of the depression that would otherwise arise. It takes a little time and reflection but it beats a day of agonized and indecisive worry; although it is not a perfect solution, given the human condition, it is about as good as they come.

Well, how about the mother-in-law coming? That kind of news, slipped in when there is no time to discuss it, may be upsetting but it also points to another problem that deserves our attention. If the communication between a husband and wife is so edgy that these unexpected announcements are always being made without previous warnings or intelligence reports, then the question of the marriage relationship itself needs to be examined. A man and woman who are gradually drifting out of phase with each other master little techniques (games, as they are called) that are meant to upset and depress each other. Husbands and wives get to be very good at playing games, knowing from their years together the exact location of each other's soft spots. A marriage like that can slowly turn into a kind of hell as the couple's communication gradually but completely disintegrates. A man cannot successfully focus on the little depressions in this kind of relationship; either he decides to get much deeper into the causes of this guerrilla warfare, or he will not have much of a marriage left and may end up communicating more clearly to his local bartender than to his wife.

As a matter of fact, if you really want to get to the bottom of your bad moods, try listening to the way in which you talk about your life and hard times to others, whether they are bartenders or your bowling buddies. Talk out loud to yourself if you must, but with some careful listening you may catch many hints of what you are really like as a person. You may even be able to siphon off the self-pity which so easily becomes a part of complaining. You will get a better picture of yourself and your own role in your depressions than you could get from a bookful of self-help philosophy. And if you listen to yourself long enough you may begin to smile, and then to laugh a little at the inconsistencies of your own position. Before you know it, you will feel much better.

BE ON THE LOOKOUT FOR
THE FOLLOWING PEOPLE

THIS is a psychological "Wanted" list, a partial compilation of individuals who are at large and who constitute a danger to our psychological well-being. Don't report them to me; I'm just warning you about them. We cannot arrest them, and, even though the temptation gets very strong at times, we cannot shoot them. As Christians we cannot just avoid them either, at least not all the time. Well, on second thought . . . .

The Teaser: Perhaps the biggest itch of all, this person plays with the feelings of others to his own advantage. He is especially dangerous when this is the only way he can get along with people. Teasing gives him great power as he leads others on, promotes their embarrassment, and withdraws quickly to a safe position with the lame but presumably effective excuse, "I was only kidding." That enables the teaser to get away with attitudes and accusations that he could never pull off if he could not hide behind the mask of the teaser. He is the master of getting you irritated enough to want to punch him in the teeth . . . but just then, he pulls back saying that you shouldn't take him so seriously. This is the moment of his greatest triumph because he leaves you with your anger and no good way to express it. Some people make a career of relating to others in this way; when they eventually discover how lonely they are it is usually too late for them to do much about it. Teasing is also a great ploy in sexual relationships. Wherever it is used, the technique is the same. The teaser, you see, is dangerously armed with sharpened wits and dulled sensitivity. Learn to protect yourself by ignoring him. And the next time you are tempted to tease somebody, think about it twice before you do.

The Know-it-all: Despite the information explosion, this character is still quite sure of himself about any and every subject under the sun. You can never tell him anything that he didn't know before you told him; and he never refrains from telling you exactly that. This latter maneuver is his favorite option in all relationships; he feels he is so damned smart that there is never any need to listen to anyone. Whether it is in science, art, or even friendship, the know-it-all is sure he can learn nothing from anyone else. It is a great but transparent and extremely annoying defense that works effectively to keep the person at a safe distance from everyone. The beauty of it is that most of this is infused knowledge, held with unshakable conviction and a large dose of invincible ignorance. He is also the kind of person who imparts massive misinformation with an air of casual certainty that causes incredible harm to other people; he is great at giving you the wrong road directions, incorrect starting times, out-of-date plane schedules, and a bullish prognostication in a bear market. Don't be deceived by the fact that he sounds authoritative; the authoritative ring in a man's voice is frequently inversely related to his possession of wisdom. If you've read or seen *Love Story* you may recall a frequently used phrase that you might well employ the next time you meet this character.

The Person Who is Too Helpful: Now it may seem strange to put a Good Samaritan on our "Wanted" list, but here he is anyway. He is just a little too helpful, perhaps a trifle unctuous in the bargain, and finds it difficult to relate to you unless he can be doing something for you. We all like things done for us but we also like to do a certain number of things for ourselves . . . and, at times, by ourselves. This character will have none of that, however, and he is forever getting in your way mixing drinks, putting the dishes in the wrong cupboards, and generally cluttering up your work area. Like a too obsequious servant he seems bent on satisfying his need to serve more than any of the real needs you may possess.

MATURITY: WHERE ARE YOU NOW
THAT I NEED YOU?

LIFE runs a contrary course for most people; that is the strange truth that properly impales the notion that maturity is a calm journey into a state of undisturbed peace. We have, of course, always known, or at least reassured ourselves with the notion, that the path of true love is not always smooth. But, a man might ask, isn't there a place where life levels off after all the uphill struggles of growing up? Does not a man who has done his best deserve at least a little quiet time to enjoy the fruits of having grown up successfully? The answer to all these musings is negative.

If you find that your challenges balloon out when you think they should be diminishing; if you feel you are too tired to get up again but realize that life never lets you sit down for very long; if maturity, or the best you have made of it, is not exactly what you have expected; well, you are probably quite healthy and normal. For these are the symptoms of maturity: not fewer problems but more of them, and more responsibility for solving them; for a time of reflective contemplation on a race well run, but a steady grind marked by a few frenzied pit stops. Yes, and to make it all worse, the mature person has a deeper sensitivity to what is happening to him; he feels life's strain more than an immature person. So the difference between an adolescent and a mature adult is not that the adult has fewer problems. Mature people—and that, of course, has a relative kind of definition—are distinguished from immature people in the way they handle their problems. Maturity seen as a sunlit, problemless plateau of life is an old and cruel myth; mature people don't get out of trouble, they just get into more of it. However, when they are truly mature, they do cope with trouble more effectively. The old and haunting dream, the tempting vision that deceives men in the measurement of their growth, presents adjustment, mental health, or personal integration (approximate synonyms abound) as the state where a man has finally got on top of all his difficulties. The grown-up, however, sees and knows that he must always respond to more problems.

The true measure of how adult we are, then, is our mode of reacting to problems; and, if our way of reacting to them causes us to taste them more painfully, it also enables us to handle them more effectively. Perhaps we can inspect ourselves and be comforted by the signs of mature instincts that we did not realize we possessed—encouraging signs that our attitudes are mature even when our woes are multiplied. For example, the mature adult minimizes his use of denial or distortion in his understanding of himself and his problems. He does not, in other words, fool himself into thinking that there is nothing wrong when there is abundant evidence of a serious difficulty. One can cite a hatful of examples of immature distortion: the parents who steadfastly deny that their child has a problem even though the signs of it are there for all to see; the alcoholic who genially insists that he has control of his problem and that he is a lovable, good guy despite the harm he is doing to others; the "cool" person who denies his own feelings in order to preserve a fragile picture of his "liberated" personality. The funny thing about these immature stances toward life, and the reason that people can often get away with them, is that they present a false front—the reflection of their passionate motivation to preserve appearances for appearances' sake. In other words, people can look good, even when they are the least mature. We may yet go down in history as the culture that hid its true worries most stylishly; and if you don't think that clothes are a good defense against the blues, go out and buy something the next time you feel down. You won't be any more mature, but you will feel better—for awhile.

The man who does not quite deny, but manages to distort, his problems gives a slightly variant picture of the same personality dynamics. By whatever turn of phrase or turn of mind, it is always somebody else's fault—the boss, the neighbor, the wife, or sometimes even the Communists. As he sees it, the world teems with wickedness and he is an innocent abroad, a victim who can only remain passive to the conspiring Fates. Oddly enough, the pose can also look good; some people get a lot of mileage out of being martyrs. And there are some who beg sympathy because they just never have had the breaks that other people get. We have always got it all wrong about them, or so they would have us believe. They pass through life ungrown, not coping with their problems in an adult manner, not even feeling life's true rhythm or its authentic depth.

So if you have the feeling that things are getting worse for you instead of better; if your difficulties are growing more, rather than less, complicated, you should be properly grateful that you are honest and open enough to define yourself and your own world accurately. Maturity and the gauge of whether you possess it lie in the way you respond to the web of interwoven problems which by mid-life seem to cover the sky itself. Maturity is the capacity to understand this and the willingness to pull yourself together in order to deal with life's problems.

ISN'T ANYBODY ELSE LONELY LIKE ME?

THE eighty-four-year-old lady in Los Angeles who recently put the above question to a newspaper reporter spoke like a modern-day Everyman. She put into words the isolated misery that grows like frost on the hearts of the lonely. There is no way to know for sure, of course, but men seem to feel that they are lonelier now than at any other time in history. That, in part, explains some of the longing we often express for the times we never knew, those times depicted so idyllically in Currier and Ives lithographs. Life still exudes from those fine-lined etchings of contented-looking people who always seem to have the time to look at and listen to and smile with each other. But where is the time for all that now? Our rapid pace and technology have produced a kind of progress, but they have helped to produce something else as well—a plaguing sense of loneliness that makes us feel fixed at isolated distances from each other like the figures in an Andrew Wyeth painting. "Isn't anybody else lonely like me?" the old lady asked. And the answer could be, "Yes, millions of us."

The tragedy of loneliness is that it is one of those human experiences that should really make us discover our kinship with each other. I have often used an elevator ride as a model for the kind of journey we make through life. We all recognize the strange and somewhat oppressive intimacy of a crowded elevator. For a moment, sinking through the shaft of a great building, we are closer to each other than we would like and we feel a tension that does not come just from the changes in gravity. We are uneasy and we are silent; we are not even sure where to look. So we hold our breaths as we silently wait for the almost blessed release when the doors part again and we can pass out into the anonymity of the "main floor crowds." It is not strange that we have all experienced these pressures; it is just sad that we experience them separately— alone, each of us—while in reality we are all going through the very same thing. That is the way it is with loneliness in our world today—a common wound felt only by humans, a suffering that should make us less than strangers. We can all say with the old lady from Los Angeles, "If you are alone, you die every day."

Perhaps loneliness, that sheer and icy fortress, yields only to an increased sensitivity to each other, a heightened recognition of our similarities rather than of our differences. But it is a strange world these days, a world of separate prides—black and white, ethnic and political, social and religious. These are the ancient strains that have kept men separate but are now emphasized to make them more aware of their individual dignity. And black *is* beautiful, there is no doubt about that. But I wonder if it would not be better to say that black is human; and so is red, and brown, and yellow as well. And they all get lonely and discouraged and look for love, as do all persons who share the inheritance of the earth. We have a claim on each other in our common humanity, in the way we discover joy or sorrow, or know loneliness. This is the awareness through which we can lift each other's loneliness.

Love, as we know well, conquers death, overcoming its curse and outlasting its pain. But love also conquers life. In many ways, that victory is just as difficult to achieve, because life wears a crooked and ambiguous smile which covers its contradictions and all its loneliness. Only a force as powerful as love can get us through a life that so often bows us to our knees and makes us cry out, "Isn't anybody else lonely like me?"

HOW NOT TO MAKE A RESOLUTION

WE hear a lot of talk today about "revolutions" but not so much anymore about "resolutions." Yet revolutions and resolutions do have some things in common. We know that both are very difficult to carry out successfully, mainly because after the first exhilarating days it is difficult to feel enthusiastic about either. And we know too (in fact it is one of the oldest truths about human nature) that both our revolutions and our resolutions have a way of transforming themselves so that things end up pretty much the way they were before either of them began.

Have you ever wondered what happened to all those resolutions you have made over the years—to lose weight, to cut down on your smoking, to be a better person in some way or other? Have you ever wondered why it was so hard to do what you thought you really wanted to do? Well, before you get into the resolution game for 1973, perhaps it would be a good idea to review some of the difficulties inherent in framing realistic resolutions.

First of all, most of us are forever trying to solve deep problems in brief and oversimplified ways. Thus, the resolution to lose weight or to stop smoking may be an oblique and unconscious attack on the reason why we eat or smoke too much in the first place. The first rule in understanding symptoms, however, is to realize that they have a functional significance that must be grasped before we can begin to rid ourselves of them. Symptoms, in other words, do something for us symbolically when we cannot handle some problem directly. That is why it is sometimes so hard to overcome a habit of overeating or excessive smoking. It is not just that we like food or tobacco; eating and smoking also relieve us of certain kinds of anxieties that we don't want to confront directly. Take away the worry-relieving symptom and you just expose yourself to the ravages of anxiety. And what do you do if you are not prepared to look into your little foible with something like insight? You turn back to eating or smoking with a vengeance, but this time you feel guilty about it, condemning yourself for having a "weakened will" or a "faulted character." And this last state of the man is much worse than the first.

Very often we make resolutions that are completely unrealistic, resolutions broken so often we should keep them in plaster casts, resolutions that seem to be recurring parts of our lives because we have dallied with them so much. Perhaps we hold on to these resolutions because they are like friendly persuaders; we make them, but we really know we won't keep them, so they are the safest and grandest resolutions of all. At other times, we make impossible resolutions because somewhere deep down we want to prove to ourselves that we really can't do certain things. There is nothing like a broken resolution to reassure us of our basic inadequacy and to excuse us from ever getting involved in life.

The roots of resolutions are varied, and only we can judge why we make, break, or even occasionally keep one of them. The best resolution is not one that sentences us to defeat or to shame ourselves. Rather it is the one that will keep us open to life's possibilities—the one that will make us ready to seize the opportunities for growth and development as persons in the days ahead. Maybe it is not so much a resolution as an attitude toward life. But the man who has it—the man with ears to hear and eyes to see—never has to make any new resolutions at all.

BEGINNING AGAIN . . .

NEW beginnings abound in the many different areas of our lives. Men must take up the frustrating little tasks that go along with the pursuit of the greatest ideals. Indeed, life at times seems to be nothing other than beginnings. Families, in nomadic North America, must begin again the search for friends in a succession of new neighborhoods. With promotions, men face the renewed challenge of proving themselves with yet another group of colleagues. The head of the house, in face of a thousand drudgeries, must carry on in getting together the tax and the mortgage money, or in finding the cash to educate the children. Parents let their children begin their own lives and find that they themselves must begin a new phase. And wise men, who think they have heard of almost all of life's problems, discover that there is always something new, something unexpected in its challenge to their response.

Even love is filled with new beginnings and repeated tests of faithfulness. These come in a hundred ways—after doubts and misunderstandings, in-law trouble and illnesses. Even those people who know and love each other very deeply are at times surprised by sudden flashes of insight that seem to be just the beginning of a new understanding of each other. Our relationships turn corners in time, and love that is truly responsible must measure up to an endless set of challenges. Real love never gets to rest on its oars in life; it is always active, always seeking a fresh understanding of things, or it isn't love at all. Real lovers have to keep working at it and there is always something new about what they face in life and in each other. But how hard it is really to make all things new in a relationship that is under stress. How hard to forgive each other for the new and often unconscious hurts we can exchange every day. Sometimes it seems easier to nurse old grudges than to face the new beginnings that forgiveness urges on us.

It is hard always to begin again, whether at trying to be better, or more loving, or to do our work with greater integrity. Easier by far to let the lines of compromise be drawn bold across life and to insulate ourselves behind them. Was there ever an age where not beginning difficult things, much less finishing them, was more exalted?

It is not surprising that a man might yearn for what he now thinks were the good old days—the days before automation and generation gaps, the splendid quiet days before the Church turned topsy-turvy on him. The Christian asks how many times he must begin again, or how many times he must be ready to let others begin again in relationship to him. Seventy times seven is not enough to count the Christian's challenges to begin anew.

That is, in fact, the real miracle of Christianity. It is set in the Testament of the New, ordered to the fresh possibilities rather than the old mistakes of life. It proclaims the availability of the Spirit who would breathe on the earth and make it a New Creation. Man is never irrevocably lost or trapped by the sins of his youth. Christianity is a faith of hope that reassures man that he can be born again, that he can be a new man in Christ Jesus. Man's redemption as well as his maturity are achieved precisely in the shifting human condition where beginning again or carrying out one's responsibilities is a daily challenge. Ever since Christ's first followers had to begin again to preach the good news at Pentecost, the Spirit has been man's strength for the new beginnings of life. The Christian life is not a die-straight road into the future. It is more like a maze, laden with wrong turns and dead ends, with surprises and difficulties. Man makes his way through it by always finding himself again, redeemed by the thousand resurrections of his spirit through which he is healed and can move forward.

The difficulties of the contemporary world and the trials of personal life seem enough to discourage the strongest of men. The temptations to drop out, or to turn aside in search of a private peace with the ever-changing world are very great. The Christian who lives by the Spirit knows that there is no end to his need to begin again but he also knows that God's promises are the guarantee that he always can begin again. That is what the resurrected life of the Spirit looks like. In living it, the Christian is a source of hope and a real sign of salvation for the whole world.